Commanding
Communications

COMMANDING COMMUNICATIONS

NAVIGATING EMERGING TRENDS IN TELECOMMUNICATIONS

Joseph Bonocore

John Wiley & Sons, Inc.

New York • Chichester • Weinheim • Brisbane • Singapore • Toronto

Library of Congress Cataloging-in-Publication Data:

Bonocore, Joseph.
    Commanding communications : navigating emerging trends in telecommunications / Joseph Bonocore.
        p. cm.
    Includes bibliographical references and index.
    ISBN 0-471-38821-1 (cloth : alk. paper)
    1. Telecommunication.   I. Title.

HE7631.B66 2000
384—dc21   00-043395

Printed in the United States of America.

10 9 8 7 6 5 4 3 2 1

Contents

Preface

"Write a book on an industry moving at the speed of light? You gotta be kidding!"

Some of my business colleagues were nothing if not blunt about the magnitude of the task that awaited me. Yet I was more determined than ever to write a book—not a technical abstract or marketing tome or statistical survey, but a comprehensive and comprehensible book—that would examine and interpret the explosive world of communications in a completely fresh and, hopefully, enlightening way. There was plenty of technical and marketing literature in circulation that nibbled on bits and pieces of the overall pie. But where was the meaningful work that attempted to digest it all and, in a cohesive and coherent way, provide a broad context for the changes that were breaking like waves all around?

As a long-time consultant to some of the largest communication companies, I had become increasingly aware of the need for such a work. Many of the discussions taking place and decisions being made around emerging communications themes and issues paid no regard to the business and regulatory environments. In talking to people in the industry I was finding that absent that overall framework, it was very difficult to cut to the tactical issues and understand the trade-offs that were often associated with those issues.

Voice-over-Internet protocol (VOIP) offers a good example. Companies and customers that are considering this emerging form of communications—which carries voice over the same high-speed packet-switching network that accommodates Internet traffic—should be looking beyond just the technology to the broader picture, which shows that for the next several years, most voice and data will ride on separate networks. There will ultimately be an integrated voice-over-Internet protocol network, but users who plan to implement the service in the near term had better be aware of the timing issues.

In an industry that is changing by the day, it soon became clear to me what I was *not* trying to accomplish. I was not trying to write a static reference work that purported to have the last word on all communications matters. Instead, my objective was to create a living, breathing book that would set forth some major directions and issues, with the full knowledge that they would change. I realized the most important thing I could hope to accomplish was not to definitively answer every question, but to provide a platform that was wide and deep enough to trigger some valuable dialogue and debate around these issues.

Who stood to benefit from this literary labor? Just about anyone with an interest, for whatever reason, in communications. I had radically altered my original plan of aiming this book primarily at members of the telecommunications industry. I realized there are many nontelecom groups whose activities impact and influence what's occurring in the industry. Beyond regulators, suppliers, information technology workers, consultants, and lawyers, there are the millions of current or prospective investors, students, job seekers, and just about anyone else with an abiding curiosity about an industry that promises to significantly change our lives in the years ahead. For all of these groups and individuals, I realized a widescreen book could help fill an information void. Even for members of the communications field who live with the drumbeat of change, a document that could provide perspective would be a valuable business tool.

My mission defined, I set forth on a task that proved to be every bit as challenging as my industry colleagues had initially warned. Rarely did a day go by without a major story involving some player, some breakthrough in the communications space that once again promised to "redefine the future." Dwarfing it all was the attempted acquisition of Sprint by MCI WorldCom for $129 billion—the "mother of all acquisitions"—until it was outmothered early in 2000 by the once-unthinkable $183 billion deal that will make Time Warner a satellite of America Online (AOL).

Indeed, much has happened since I first started preparing this book. The good news is that the preponderance of breaking events were either consistent with what I had already written, or clarified points that might not have been so obvious at the start of my endeavor. For example, the prevailing wisdom had been that the industry would fall out along the lines of broadband service carriers and wireless service carriers. The proposed MCI WorldCom-Sprint megadeal, however, precipitated a basic rethinking of the issue, and the new calculus suggests that the major players going forward will indeed require both broadband and wireless capabilities to remain competitive.

In addition, when I began this book, it was difficult to foresee the overnight sensation that data over wireless would become. Since its introduction several years ago, wireless data has had to wrestle with slow transmission speeds and spotty geographic coverage. Moreover, users had to settle for a few lines of text on a tiny screen, and the number of web sites formatted for wireless access was extremely limited.

While it's still several years away from offering the rich web experience that desktop and laptop systems offer, wireless data has suddenly come to life and is making its robust presence known with the help of new-age devices like the PalmPilot and the heavy promotion of Sprint PCS's new wireless data service. To appreciate the full potential of this technology, one has to look no further than the pilot tests Nokia is running in Europe with its advanced wireless phones. Shoppers who have just made a purchase, for example, can aim the device at the store cash register and trigger an instantaneous transfer of money via wireless connection from their bank account to that of the store. No need for money, or even a credit or debit card. Your phone *is* your cash. Imagine the possibilities.

Even the biggest communications bombshell to drop since I began preparing this book — AOL's proposed purchase of Time Warner—sorted neatly with the structural framework (past, present, and future) I had laid out for the industry, and confirmed in my mind that I was on the right track. The marriage of new content and old content implicit in the deal creates the world's most formidable cache of print, film, music, and television programming. Time Warner's acquisition of the EMI Group only two weeks after the AOL deal, which created the world's largest record company, drove home the point. In merging with Time Warner, however, AOL is not only becoming the 20,000-pound content gorilla, it's gaining desperately needed broadband access via Time Warner's cable network, which reaches into some 13 million American households. Not wanting to be left at the altar with no distribution options, AOL also has deals cooking with regional telephone companies for DSL access and with Hughes Electronics Corporation for satellite TV.

But here's the rub: I believe that AOL chief Stephen Case is looking well beyond what's already on his radar screen, to a future deal with either AT&T or MCI WorldCom that would give the Internet service provider the meganetwork access it needs to remain competitive. If and when this happens, it will be another compelling example of content merging with conduit—a fundamental industry movement that is well under way and that promises to touch off other titanic alliances and takeovers in the next few years. The coupling of AOL and Time Warner certainly puts the new media giant in a much stronger bargaining position with the likes of conduit leaders AT&T and MCI WorldCom to reach some kind of accord.

To be sure, the future shape of the communications industry is one of the most fascinating aspects of any industry examination. The outcome will determine how entire industry segments play out. For example, which device will emerge the winner in the drive to put communications at the epicenter of our lives: the telephone, the computer, or the television? I personally believe it will be a device that combines the functionality of all three. Will the consolidation mania sweeping the industry result in a Darwinian landscape ruled by industry goliaths? Size will continue to be critical, but I believe we are about to see another industry phenomenon: an explosion of small, specialized communications companies that will become virtual global carriers overnight through their ability to tie into the meganetworks of the industry powerhouses.

Giving readers a framework for understanding how events like the preceding, and many more, might unfold and impact the industry and, eventually, their own lives is precisely what *Commanding Communications* is aimed at. But like the industry itself, this book is very much a work in progress. There is always another chapter to be written. My best advice to readers . . . stay tuned!

Acknowledgments

I'd like to pay special thanks to three people without whose hard work and dedication — days, nights, and weekends — this book would never have made it to press. They are:

Hubert Vaz-Nayak, KPMG's former director of marketing for the communications industry, currently the vice president of marketing at Eclipse Networks. Thanks to his extensive background in and knowledge of the communications industry, he not only contributed significantly to the content of the book, but also expertly managed the entire project, from start to finish. Hubert was thorough to a fault, handling an avalanche of details and serving as my sounding board on issues and ideas that continually came to the fore in the course of preparing this book.

Randy Young, whose considerable writing and research skills were an indispensable part of this huge undertaking. Randy worked closely with Hubert and me to distill a wealth of material into a highly readable form that I felt extremely comfortable with.

Kami Sterling, my very able assistant who has been with me through thick and thin over the past few years. Kami took a particularly active role in this project, helping me compile and sort my random thoughts, and tending to the endless chores that needed to be done, precisely when they needed to be done.

I would like to also thank my devoted and loving wife, Phyllis, who has supported me in everything that I have wanted to do over many years, including the time and effort that was necessary to complete this book. I would also like to especially thank my three grown children — Joseph, Kristen, and Michael — for their support and for putting up with my endless bantering about the book and the hours of calls made to discuss the book with the team. I could not have been blessed with a better family than the one I have.

Chapter *1*

The Digital Dream Takes Shape

Five-thirty A.M., and once again the Boston Pops is rousing me from a deep slumber. The music is streaming from the TV perched on my dresser, heralding the start of another jam-packed business day. As my eyes start to unseal, they're greeted with my morning information digest playing across the TV monitor. First come quotes on the stocks I'm watching for my portfolio, followed by the sports scores and a brief news summary of things that matter to me. I'm relieved to see the planet is still in relatively good shape; while I slept, the foreign stock markets remained stable and my beloved 49ers managed to pull off a last-minute upset in Monday Night Football.

As I head for the shower and the screen loses "sight" of me, my itinerary for the day converts from visual to voice readout, beginning with my 6:35 limo trip to the airport, followed by a 7:35 flight to Chicago to make a two o'clock meeting with a group of business partners.

I love this kind of planning and organization—so efficient! But it's about to come to a grinding halt. En route to the airport, my Internet phone beeps me with an update on my flight. I cringe at what I see on the display: It's been canceled. Having been through this drill before, I know it's time to put myself in the hands of my IT genie.

In the time it's taken me to look at the information on

my small display, the software from my online office organizer has accessed my travel profile and my day's itinerary, including the people I'm scheduled to meet with, and automatically booked me on an alternate airline and flight that will get me into Chicago only 30 minutes behind schedule. My calendar has also been revised, and the people who are slated to be at the two o'clock meeting notified via e-mail. Their schedules have also automatically adjusted.

Relieved of those time-consuming chores, I sink back into the limo's Corinthian leather and whip out my Palm-Pilot. No need to boot up; it's always on. Through the device's built-in high-speed, wireless modem, I'm able to log onto my firm's intranet to the collaborative section of the project that's about to unfold today. Looks like my partners in Chicago have been pretty busy over the past few hours, and with good reason. The agenda for our meeting today has significantly changed—at the client's request. I carefully review the revisions that have been made to our multimedia presentation and, with a flurry of keystrokes, make some changes and suggestions of my own. The irony then occurs to me: so much "collaborative" work going on without my ever speaking to another team member. By the time I arrive at the airport, a final version of our presentation is ready for review. My IT genie has once again come through with flying colors!

Fast-forward eight hours. Our meeting with the client is a success despite all these manmade obstacles. Which leaves only one unfinished piece of business: finding a good restaurant to take our client to. Italian being their preference (no arguments here), I get on my Internet phone once again and call my all-purpose, private directory service, which has in its database the names and ratings of every Italian restaurant in Chicago. An automated attendant takes my request via speech recognition, and begins processing the information.

While visions of veal picata dance in my head, a commercial satellite in orbit 100 miles *above* my head locks onto my precise physical location. Building on that information, the automated directory system assembles a list of four top-tier Italian eateries within a five-mile radius of our office building. In seconds, the automated attendant is back on the line feeding me this information. I like the sound of one trattoria in particular I've always wanted to visit. And with that, the synthesized voice asks if I would care to see their menu. Sure, I reply, and the screen on my Internet phone comes alive with the restaurant's mouth-watering fare, complete with prices. Bingo!

But wait, my friendly directory service isn't finished yet. The attendant wants to know if it can alert the restaurant to our impending arrival, and perhaps have a table waiting. Sounds great, I reply, and the service finishes the transaction by displaying on my screen directions to the restaurant.

A bit far-fetched, you say? Not at all. The core technologies to bring this tableau and every one of the preceding transactions to life already exist. They reside in a clutch of high-speed communications networks embracing wireline and wireless technologies—technologies that are reconfiguring our lives in ways that just 10 years ago would have been unimaginable. For one thing, they're turning upside-down the time-honored notion of workspace and personal space, replacing them with a seamless work-leisure environment in which we'll actually have greater flexibility than ever before to do what we want to do, when we want to do it. Want to play golf in the daytime and work till 2 a.m.? Or perhaps stage a videoconference from the comfort of your living room, using the eight hours you saved in round-trip travel time to finish a budget analysis for the boss, *plus* take the family out to dinner?

Thanks to the exhilarating new age of communications that's dawning, we'll no longer be confined to the office or to the traditional nine-to-five work window. We'll have the ability to link with anyone, anywhere, anytime. This will mean greater convenience and, just as important, it will mean better access to the information and ideas we need to enhance our performance, and our lives. As business after business is discovering, survival today really does depend on who can turn information to their advantage in the quickest and most imaginative ways.

■ EMERGING TRENDS

Convergence is the battle cry of the new communications revolution. At the same time communications companies are expanding their capabilities, they're bringing them together in a host of ways to the decided benefit of business and residential users. Voice, data, Internet access, cable TV, and multimedia are converging on the same network as carriers seek to provide customers with convenient, one-stop shopping. Networks and software are also converging and, in the future, it will be virtually impossible to tell where the intelligent network ends and its software cousin begins. Even communications service providers are converging, swallowing each other up and engineering partnerships and alliances, as they attempt to fashion themselves into sleek new models able to gain the best competitive position on the unfolding communications megahighway.

In this world of monumental change, challenges and opportunities, I see the following bold outlines taking shape:

➤ The intelligent network—an interactive medium that provides users with an unprecedented range of information, applications and services—will reign supreme. This thinking network, as I call it, will virtually replace the so-called dumb network, which simply transports information between end points, although dumb network advocates insist that its ability to deliver enhanced user control and better value makes *it* the network of the future.

➤ Technological advances in bandwidth and routers on the new high-capacity networks will reduce the cost of providing communications services by at

Global Crossing

There are few better examples of today's high-octane tele-communications upstart than Global Crossing. Founded in 1997 by the Pacific Capital Group, Bermuda-based Global Crossing is the world's first independent provider of global long-distance telecom services. The company is currently building an undersea digital fiber optic cable system and terrestrial backhaul capacity to reach the world's top 50 telecommunications traffic cities. In addition to four planned undersea cables (the first U.S.-U.K. cable has been completed), Global Crossing has announced plans for a 7,200-kilometer terrestrial pan-European network and a 1,200-kilometer terrestrial network in Japan. With these resources, the company will serve as a carriers' carrier, selling capacity to other telephone companies and large businesses for Internet and data services.

With former AT&T executive Leo Hindery at the helm, Global Crossing's plans to quickly catapult into the big leagues of business communication by merging with U S WEST were thwarted by Qwest Communications, which stepped in at the eleventh hour to win a highly publicized bidding war. Global Crossing ended up instead with Frontier Communications, the American long-distance telephone company, as part of an $11 billion deal.

Given the company's resolute focus on the future, however, it's unlikely the tussle with US WEST did much to derail Global Crossing's plans for unbridled growth in the decade ahead.

least 70% over the next five years, driving down prices and generating an unprecedented demand for network capacity by consumers and businesses.

➤ A virtual global network is emerging—an Internet protocol (IP)–driven network of open, flexible architecture that allows networks anywhere in the world to link with any other network so that users enjoy seamless, unsurpassed access to information and services.

➤ Voice communications will be provided free of charge to many business and residential customers, and traditional telephone companies will have to change quickly to data, video, and multimedia services to maintain their current revenue levels.

➤ The "last mile" leading up to the home may be the most hotly contested battleground right now for telecom companies, but the "extra mile" that runs *through* the home has the potential to be equally lucrative thanks to a potpourri of emerging teleliving applications.

➤ Incremental change will not be the prescription for success in the new age of communications. Service providers who don't target massive change in areas like customer service and business and operating support systems will find themselves being buried alive by more aggressive and savvy competitors.

➤ Strategic alliances with the right partners will be virtually essential for companies if they expect to be viable players in the national, global, or intelligent network arenas.

➤ Major content companies like Walt Disney, Viacom, and AOL Time Warner will form mega-alliances with communications providers like MCI WorldCom and AT&T, giving them the ability to provide the kind of flexible, interactive programming they could never hope to achieve on their own. As these strategic alliances take shape, the major TV networks like CBS (owned by Viacom) and ABC (owned by Walt Disney) will be relegated to single all-news/information channels on their parent company's programming lineup.

➤ While consolidations will continue to grab the headlines in the near term, we are on the verge of another explosion: small, specialized communications companies that will enjoy the same global reach as the industry giants thanks to their ability to link to the meganetworks of these large carriers.

■ THE NEW TELECOM TOPOGRAPHY

To those of us who remember the not-so-distant past, when telecommunications service was provided by a single regulated monopoly and long distance was about as adventurous as it got, the advance to today's environment is akin to jumping through the looking glass. Consolidations. Convergence. Deregulation. Internet protocol. The last mile. Cable modems. What's this all about, anyway? It's about fundamental change that is shaking the industry to its core — change that is giving birth to a sleek new communications megahighway that promises to provide the pulsebeat for the new millennium.

The first rumblings of change were touched off by the breakup of the mighty Bell System in 1984, the result of a U.S. Department of Justice antitrust suit. That action left seven separate local telephone companies — variously known as the Regional Bell Operating Companies, RBOCs, or Baby Bells — and one unaffiliated long-distance company, AT&T. (See Figure 1.1 for the changes that have occurred with these companies since break up of AT&T.) Even so, telecommunications in the United States continued to be highly regulated and local telephone service was still the province of monopolies overseen by state public utility commissions.

Gradually, the domestic long-distance market became more competitive as MCI and Sprint entered the arena. Later on, they would be joined by a new wave of competitors like LCI, WilTel, IXC, Level 3, Qwest, Williams, Frontier, and numerous resellers determined to claim their share of the marketplace. Fueling the expansion of these long-distance networks spanning regional, state, and international borders was the exceptional growth in traffic: about 5 to 7%

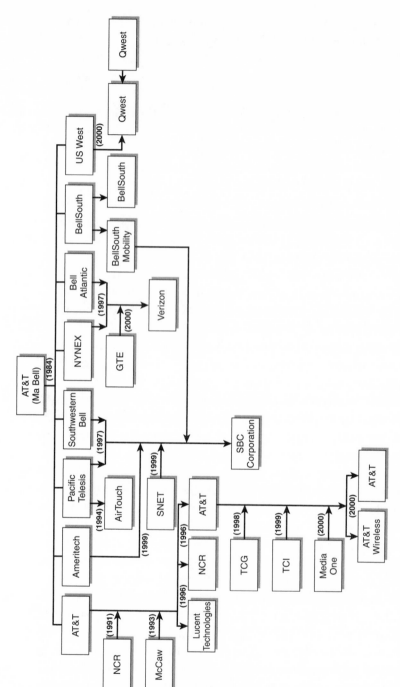

Figure 1.1 AT&T Divestiture and Beyond

Note: This diagram indicates only the major acquisitions and divestitures AT&T and the regional Bells gave gone through since 1984.

Source: Eclipse Networks Research

annually for voice and, more recently, well over 100% for data thanks to the Internet explosion.

Changes in long-distance service at the global level have been no less impressive. According to *Telegeography,* new entrants around the world won over 11% of the monstrous international long-distance market from 1990 to 1997. And as more and more markets worldwide deregulate, Merrill Lynch believes that penetration figure will climb to over 20% within the next five years.

The magnitude of change in the United States is starkly reflected in AT&T's loss of long-distance market share from nearly 90% in 1984 to under 50% today (see Figure 1.2). According to the FCC, numerous newcomers with tiny individual market shares raised their collective share from 12.3% in 1993 to nearly 20% of the total long-distance market in 1997.

At long last, the competitive genie was out of the bottle, paving the way for the next landmark decree: the Telecommunications Act of 1996. The first major overhaul of Federal Communications Commission (FCC) law since the agency was created in 1934, the act was designed to provide a major stimulus to local telephone competition. The FCC attempted to accomplish this by requiring the incumbent local telephone companies (mainly the RBOCs) to open their networks so competitors could interconnect (in other words, exchange traffic) with the incumbents and even lease elements of the network that the new entrants lacked, such as switches and customer lines. To give this edict even sharper teeth, the Telecommunications Act continued to bar the incumbents from the long-distance market in their serving areas until they had met a laundry list of requirements designed to conclusively prove they had opened their local markets to competition.

The revolution in local telephone service that the Telecommunications Act was supposed to herald has been painfully slow in coming. In fact, it took nearly four years from the act's passage for Bell Atlantic to win approval for long-distance service in New York, the first such approval

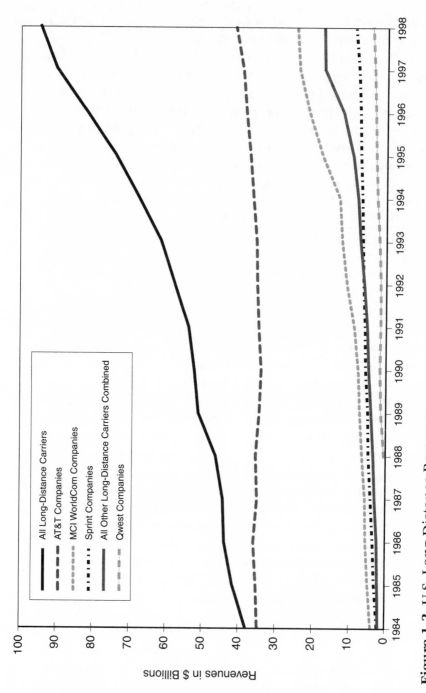

Figure 1.2 U.S. Long Distance Revenues

Source: Federal Communications Commission

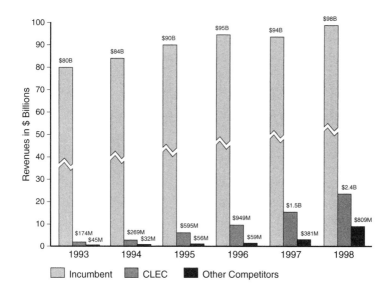

Figure 1.3 CLEC Share of Local Service Revenues

Source: Federal Communications Commission

granted to an RBOC, and nearly as long for AT&T, MCI WorldCom, and other long-haul carriers to begin selling local telephone service in the same market.

Though decried by many industry experts, the Telecommunications Act of 1996 has touched off some noteworthy changes in the competitive landscape. For example:

➤ An onrush of new companies known as competitive local exchange carriers, or CLECs, has entered the wireline local services market, providing both switched voice and high-speed data services to customers. The CLECs have invested billions of dollars and, according to recent figures, are gaining between 600,000 and 700,000 customer lines per quarter, most of them high-value business customers (see Figure 1.3). CLECs embrace both resellers of incumbent phone carriers' services and companies offering services over their own network facilities.

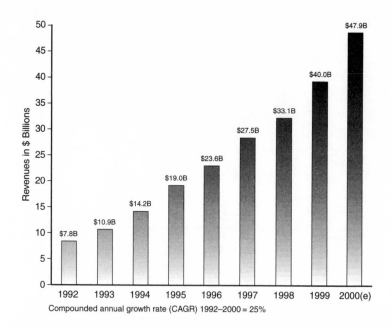

Figure 1.4 U.S. Wireless Industry: Annual Revenues

Sources: Cellular Telecommunications Industry Association, Standard & Poor's

➤ Increased capacity and competition following the Telecommunications Act have served to further fan the growth of wireless communications. By the end of 1999, there were over 86 million cellular sub-scribers in the United States — more than one in four adults. That's nearly 60% higher than in 1996 and five times the number in 1993. What's more, wireless telephony has become a $30 billion industry (see Figure 1.4), employing over 160,000 people.

■ THE GROWTH OF WIRELINE AND WIRELESS

A sign of the changing times is that the word *telecommunications* is fast being retired. Traditional telecommunications companies that provided basic voice and data services are morphing into *communications* companies with the ability to offer now, or in the future, a full panoply of services, from local and long distance to wireless and cable programming to Internet access and multimedia. Making these services possible is a range of technologies—some old, some new—that are forever changing how we look at communications. These technologies fit into the general categories of *wireline* and *wireless.*

➤ Wireline Communications

Even with the rapid growth of wireless, wireline continues to be the dominant form of communications, accounting for about 80% not only of the more than $800 billion in global telecommunication revenues annually, but of the $300 billion-plus domestic U.S. market as well (see Figure 1.5). And within wireline, fiber optics has become the medium of choice to satisfy the demand for greater bandwidth (the amount of data that can be carried by a channel) required for modern-day applications like video, graphics, and multimedia. Worldwide spending on fiber optic equipment reached $12 billion in 1998, and is expected to more than double to $25 billion by 2002 (see Figure 1.6). In the vanguard of this infrastructure development across the United States and overseas are companies like MCI WorldCom, Qwest, Level 3 Communications, and Global Crossing. Sprint has spent $2 billion in recent years building a packet-switched broadband network, while Qwest is putting in place a hybrid system with both circuit- and packet-switching capabilities for voice and data.

A growing number of communications operators believe that Internet protocol (IP) will become the global communications standard by 2004 for transmitting digital information over fiber optic trunk lines. IP-based networks transmit data in packets that are each encoded with an address and reassembled when they get to their destination to create the entire message. Wireline service providers are currently scrambling to provide voice-over-Internet protocol (VOIP) services, but the existing quality and reliability have a long way to go before they can be rolled out to the general public.

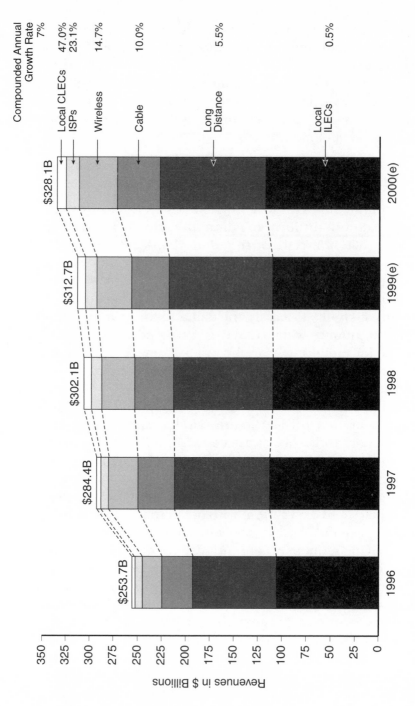

Figure 1.5 Size of the U.S. Telecommunications Market

Sources: CTIA, Decision Resources, DLJ (Donaldson Luftkin Jenerette), Merrill Lynch, Paul Kagan Associates, SFCG (San Francisco Consulting Group) Analysis

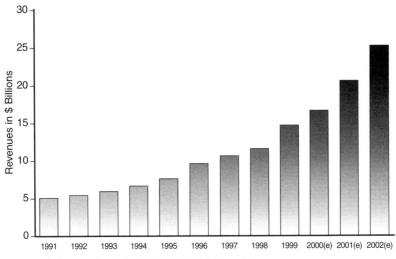

Compounded Annual Growth Rate (CAGR) 1991–2002 = 16%

Figure 1.6 Fiber Optic Spending

Sources: Telecommunications Industry Association, Multimedia Association

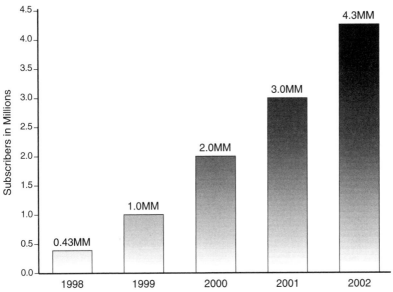

Compounded Annual Growth Rate (CAGR) 1998–2000 = 78%

Figure 1.7 U.S. Cable Modem Subscribers

Source: "Cable Modems vs. DSL: Dispelling the Myths," *The Yankee Report: Consumer Communications,* November, 1998, 9.

Level 3's IP Foray

Level 3 Communications has seen the future—and is translating that vision into the first international Internet protocol (IP)–based network to be built from the ground up. IP is fast emerging as the communications standard for transmitting digital information globally over fiber optic lines.

Focused on the business market, Level 3 will provide a full range of communications services—from local and long distance to data transmission and Internet access—across the United States, Europe, and Asia. Level 3 expects its network, which will be completed in phases over the next four to six years, to serve 70 to 80 cities around the world through its own local and long-distance facilities. The network will be built through a combination of construction, purchase, and leasing of assets, and is designed to be more adaptable to future technological upgrades than are the current older and less flexible competitive networks. (In order to support the launch of its services and develop a customer base in advance of completing its own network, the company has begun offering services in 17 U.S. cities, as well as London and Frankfurt, over leased lines.)

Level 3's allegiance to IP is driven by its belief in the

Cable networks are wireline structures that consist of both fiber optic and coaxial cable. These broadband networks, which for years have transmitted cable TV programming, are now being expanded to embrace Internet access and voice telephony. More than a million people currently access the Internet via high-speed cable modems, with that number expected to increase to 4.3 million by 2002, according to the Yankee Group (see Figure 1.7).

➤ Wireless Communications

Throughout much of the world, wireless has become a runaway train of growth. Consider the numbers. Global spending on wireless services totaled $163 billion in 1998, and is

fundamental shift now occurring in the communications industry—a shift away from the traditional circuit-switched networks that were designed primarily for voice communications to advanced packet-switched networks using the Internet protocol. This new technology permits the movement of information at a much lower cost because packet switching makes more efficient use of network capacity. Unlike its competitors, Level 3 has no investment in circuit-switched technology.

Level 3 Communications was founded in 1985 as Kiewit Diversified Group (KDG), a wholly owned subsidiary of Peter Kiewit Sons, Inc., a 114-year-old construction, mining, information services, and communications company headquartered in Omaha, Nebraska. In January 1998, KDG announced it was changing its name to Level 3 Communications; three months later, Level 3 became an independent corporation following its separation from Peter Kiewit Sons.

Among the company's greatest strengths is a strong and capable management team, led by CEO Jim Crowe, whose colleagues share an abiding passion: to build and operate one of the most technologically advanced fiber optic networks in the world.

projected to rise to $313 billion by 2002 (see Figure 1.8). Wireless traffic, which currently constitutes only about 2% of the total telecom volume, is expected to hit 18% in 2002 and 30% within 10 years. In the last three years, the number of wireless subscribers has tripled, with more than one-third of all new telecom customers weighing in with wireless. At the start of the new millennium, the worldwide population of cell phones stood at a robust 427 million.

In the United States, the term *cellular* has historically been used to refer to analog phone service. Today, its chief advantage is that it's available just about everywhere. But since analog cellular represents early technology, it's starting to lose market share rapidly to advanced digital cellular and PCS (personal communication services; see Figure 1.9). (The only significant difference between digital

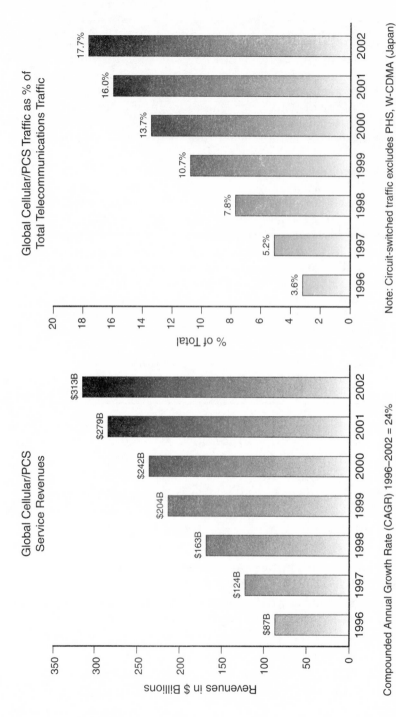

Figure 1.8 Global Wireless Market Forecasts

Source: The Yankee Group, 1998

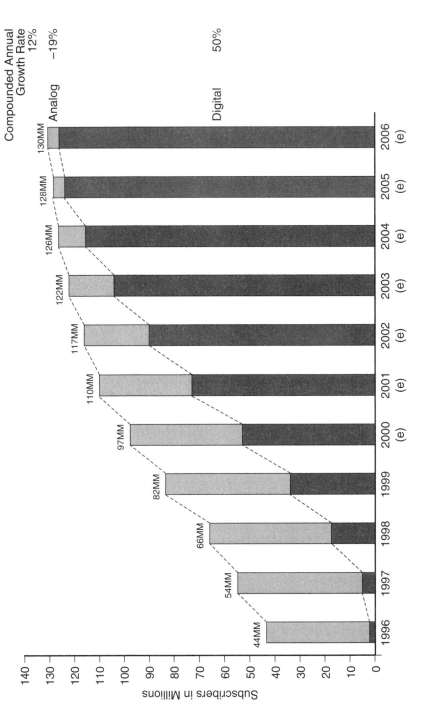

Figure 1.9 U.S. Wireless Subscribers: Analog versus Digital

Source: The Strategis Group

cellular and PCS is the frequencies they operate in. In fact, several wireless companies tend to use a combination of cellular and PCS frequencies to provide ubiquitous coverage: The phones have the ability to jump between the frequencies when necessary.) Digital cellular is much clearer than its predecessor; however, it is not yet universally available. This will in all likelihood change as the result of the recent agreement by 40 of the world's largest wireless operators and suppliers to standardize on third-generation (3G) digital code division multiple access (CDMA) technology. The net effect is a major step toward a completely digital wireless network that would give customers global roaming capabilities not currently available because of the technical differences between wireless operators and service providers.

The Yankee Group predicts that by 2003, there will be more than 66 million digital cellular users in the United States, compared to 16 million analog subscribers. PCS subscribers could total 40 million by 2003, according to the Cellular Telecommunications Industry Association (CTIA). Options such as e-mail and paging make digital wireless particularly attractive. Almost all the wireless players now offer digital service.

To be sure, wireless is no longer just about voice. In the early 1990s, the cellular industry introduced CDPD — cellular digital packet data service. The service did not achieve any noticeable market acceptance, however, due to a combination of factors, ranging from the industry's inability to understand the service to inadequate investment in the area. In 1999, the network equipment manufacturers decided that wireless data was the next frontier to tackle. With excellent marketing timing, Sprint introduced its own wireless data services, backed by a sizable marketing budget, and the field has taken off like a heat-seeking missile. The swelling ranks of Internet-ready wireless data subscribers globally are expected to soar to over 1 billion by 2004 (see Figure 1.10). The Yankee Group predicts that one-third of all large U.S. firms will provide wireless Internet access to their field and sales employees. And while wireless data

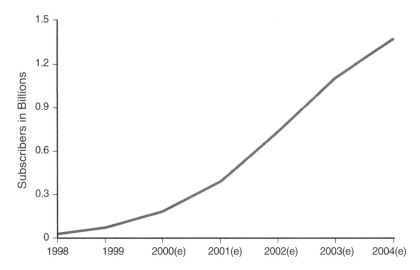

Figure 1.10 Global Wireless Web Users

Source: International Data Corporation

technology must still overcome a number of hurdles, major advances are on the horizon. A group of large wireless service providers — including AT&T, British Telecommunications, Ericsson, and Nortel Networks — has announced it will collaborate on developing a next-generation, IP packet-based network designed for high-speed data communication. This network will support such devices as Samsung Electronics' Internet phone, a cellular phone and personal digital assistant with Internet access and a touch screen for sending text messages. It also features a PC data interface for remotely accessing information stored on a hard drive. In addition, wireless operators will soon start rolling out a data transmission standard known as general packet radio service, or GPRS. The new standard will enable cell phone users to remain connected to the web every minute their devices are on.

Satellite is another form of wireless communications poised to grab a chunk of the broadband market. Total global sales in the commercial satellite industry were nearly $66 billion in 1998, up 15% from the prior year. U.S.-

RCN Carves Out a Consumer Niche

RCN Corporation is focused on a telecom segment that Chairman David McCourt believes has been long overlooked and undervalued by the industry: the residential customer. Ranked second on a list of the 100 most innovative telecommunications companies in America by *Forbes ASAP* in April 1999, RCN is a lean and aggressive provider leaving its mark as a competitive local exchange carrier (CLEC) and Internet service provider (ISP).

RCN is well positioned to succeed in the local exchange market through a $12 billion high-capacity fiber optic network the communications upstart is building to compete with the nation's cable TV and local phone company giants. That network has been initially — and shrewdly — targeted at some of the most desirable urban neighborhoods within the Boston to Washington, D.C., corridor. The company has also begun developing an advanced fiber network in the San Francisco to San Diego corridor. Generally, RCN has defined its market niche as neighborhoods with high-density housing and favorable demographics. Indeed, when its networks are completed by 2008, RCN will cover only 6% of the country, but will compete for no less than 44% of its telecommunications traffic.

based companies accounted for over $30 billion of that volume. Overall, the global satellite business is expected to drive $150 billion in annual revenues from telephony and high-speed Internet access by 2008.

That may be wishful thinking, however, if the industry doesn't attempt to get its act together. As *The New York Times* stated, "Rarely, it seems, has an industry been blessed with so much potential and cursed with so many problems." Among the latter are rocket failures, manufacturing glitches, and soaring insurance premiums that have made it more difficult and costly to get satellites into the sky. In addition, satellite communications often perform poorly in densely populated areas, like cities, due to buildings and other sig-

RCN's strategy is clear: to become the leading single-source provider of voice, TV, and Internet access to its residential customers through individual or bundled service options, while offering superior customer service and competitive pricing. The company is already the largest regional ISP in the Northeast, with over 500,000 Internet connections, thanks to a battery of acquisitions. They include Ultranet Communications and Erols Internet in February 1998, Interport Communications in June 1998, and Javanet the following month. RCN's primary service offerings in the Internet field are 56-Kbps dial-up and high-speed cable modem access.

The Princeton, New Jersey–based provider has also entered into a number of strategic alliances to ramp up for the future. These include construction agreements with Level 3 Communications, which will provide RCN with a cross-country fiber backbone allowing connectivity to major Internet connection points in the United States; an agreement with Qwest Communications to utilize that company's fiber lines to tie together RCN's local networks from Boston to Washington; and a long-term lease arrangement with MFS WorldCom to use its fiber optic network in New York City and Boston.

nal-hampering barriers. Another major problem for satellite providers has been signing up the required number of subscribers to make the service profitable. Iridium L.L.C., the satellite pioneer heavily backed by Motorola, graphically illustrates the point. After spending more than $5 billion over the past decade to create a global network of 66 low-orbiting satellites, the company had enticed a meager 20,000 subscribers. In August of 1999 they filed for bankruptcy protection and eventually terminated service in 2000.

It seems likely that if any satellite venture is going to succeed in the short term, it will have to provide broadband data communications, including Internet access and videoconferencing, rather than voice. Boeing, for one, is developing a

satellite system to provide Internet service to airline pas-
sengers. One of the most ambitious projects is Teledesic's
satellite-based Internet-in-the-sky network, whose backers
include William Gates of Microsoft and cellular phone mag-
nate Craig McCaw. Teledesic envisions a $10 billion system
of 288 satellites that would begin operating in 2004.

To be sure, the satellite industry faces formidable challenges, not only technically but in the form of mounting
competition from cable and telephone companies seeking
to provide customers with high-speed access. Nonetheless,
there appears to be plenty of elbow room for each technology to succeed in the decade ahead.

■ THE INDUSTRY'S POWERHOUSES

If the communications industry is moving more and more
toward the concept of "general store," which companies,
then, will be the strongest, most dominant proprietors?
Given the investment required, it's clear that only the very
largest players will be able to offer customers a full range of
wireline and wireless services over a seamless network, or
be able to achieve the economies of scale needed to provide
competitive pricing for their services on local, national, and
international scales. Based on my analysis, I believe six
companies are currently taking the steps necessary to become full-service global communication providers. They are:

> ➤ *AT&T.* This telecom titan gets credit for taking the
> competitive battle to a new front, away from the tra-
> ditional telephone network and onto cable tele-
> vision systems through its acquisitions of
> Tele-Communications, Inc. (TCI) and MediaOne
> (see Figure 1.11 for AT&T's acquisitions). In the pro-
> cess, A&T, under the firm leadership of C. Michael
> Armstrong, not only stands to become the country's
> largest cable operator, but a good bet to crack the

Company Transacted with	Year	Service Area	Type of Transaction
MediaOne	2000	Cable	Acquisition
American Cellular	1999	Wireless	Acquisition
Vanguard Cellular	1999	Wireless	Acquisition
Rogers Cantel	1999	Wireless	Investment
Honolulu Cellular	1999	Wireless	Acquisition
Comcast	1999	Cable	Marketing Agreement
Lenfest Communications	1999	Cable	Acquisition
IBM Global Network Services	1999	Networking	Acquisition
MetroNet	1999	Local Access	Merger
Time Warner	1999	Cable	Joint Venture
Tele-Communications, Inc. (TCI) (includes 41% of @Home)	1998	Cable	Merger
Teleport Communications Group (TCG)	1988	CLEC	Merger
McCaw Cellular/LIN Cellular	1994	Wireless	Acquisition

Figure 1.11 AT&T's Key North American Transactions & Investments

Source: AT&T

Regional Bell Operating Companies' dominance of the $110 billion local telephone market. AT&T's strategy involves a radical change in emphasis from long-distance service with all its cutthroat competition and shrinking margins to a more balanced cache of bundled services, everything from high-speed Internet connections and wireless to local and long-distance telephony to communications consulting. Whether Michael Armstrong can pull off his audacious plan for transforming the telecom behemoth is anyone's guess at this point. Cable, after all, is still an unproven medium when it comes to telephony.

AT&T is working on many other fronts, however, to develop promising new consumer and business markets. It engineered a $11.3 billion merger with Teleport Communications Group, the largest independent provider of local phone service to businesses; undertook a joint venture with British Telecommunications (BT) to link the world's leading 100 economic centers; completed an AT&T-BT investment in Japan Telecom as well as an AT&T agreement with NTT; and acquired for $5 billion IBM's global data network.

➤ *MCI WorldCom.* Through its numerous acquisitions of Sprint and other considerable assets, this telecom goliath is clearly *the* industry force to be reckoned with in the new millennium. MCI WorldCom is well along in its hard-driving strategy: to become the leading provider to customers, especially businesses, of a full range of communications services, from wireless to Internet access to international calling. It already operates from a position of strength in the fields of data transmission and Internet access. The addition of Sprint would have made the company a formidable wireless contender and would have been a fitting cap to a string of deals that have seen MCI WorldCom under Chairman Bernie Ebbers grow by leaps and bounds (see Figure 1.12). They include the

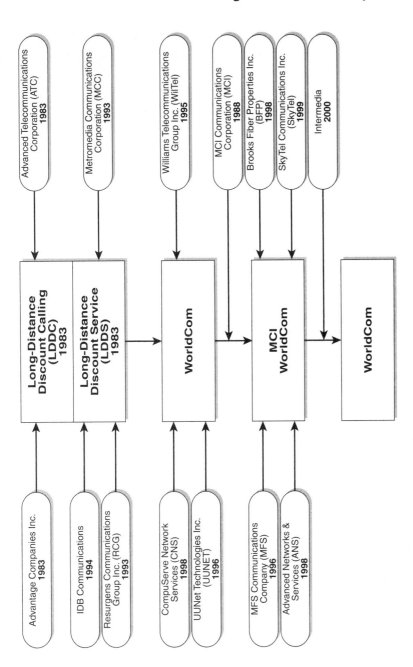

Figure 1.12 Evolution of WorldCom

Source: Eclipse Networks Research

purchase of Brooks Fiber, which brought 40 new local exchange markets to the company, and the CompuServe merger and purchase of ANS from AOL, which bolstered the company's Internet and system integration capabilities. The company is itself the product of the 1998 merger of WorldCom and MCI, whose collective assets include UUNet (the large Internet Service Provider), and MFS Communications Company, which owns local network access facilities in and around major U.S. cities. These properties have enabled MCI WorldCom to focus heavily on self-reliance, which translates into end-to-end control of its own fiber optic network, both domestically and globally.

➤ *SBC Communications.* This most profitable and largest of the Baby Bells has been working hard to "bulk up" as it prepares to go head-to-head with AT&T to offer customers integrated packages of communication services. The company's acquisition since 1997 of Pacific Telesis Group, Southern New England Telephone Company, and Ameritech Corporation — the last a $72 billion deal creating the nation's largest local telephone company with roughly 55 million telephone lines in 13 states — is a critical part of that strategy. So are its merger with Bell South Mobility and partnership with DirecTV, the nation's biggest satellite broadcaster, which adds television to the roster of wireline and wireless services it intends to bring to customers. The real prize for SBC, however, will be its entry into the long-distance marketplace. SBC's transformation comes none too soon: industry analysts believe that giants like AT&T and MCI WorldCom could siphon off 25% of its local phone business by 2003, including many lucrative business accounts.

➤ *Verizon Communications.* This Baby Bell, known earlier as Bell Atlantic, first increased its footprint by acquiring NYNEX in August of 1997. Through its entry into long-distance service and merger with GTE, Verizon Communications, already the largest wireline local telephone company in the United States, is preparing to become one of the five or six dominant communications players worldwide. Its focus, at least initially, is on serving the consumer marketplace. Verizon Communications would offer up control of one-third of all local phone service in the United States. In striking a recent deal with one-time adversary Vodafone AirTouch P.L.C., Verizon Communications also acquired a national cellular footprint as well as the scale to compete against powerhouses AT&T and Sprint in the burgeoning wireless market. On the broadband front, Verizon Communications is counting on its rollout of digital subscriber line (DSL) technology to counter AT&T's cable onslaught. One way the company hopes to drive consumer acceptance of DSL is through its marketing arrangement with America Online to package high-speed transport along with the popular AOL portal.

➤ *Deutsche Telekom.* Failing in its bid to acquire Telecom Italia, this large German carrier still has its sights set on becoming a global power with a commensurate range of services. The firm is currently in the process of completing its acquisition of Voice Stream — a large U.S. wireless service provider — that will give it a footprint in North America. But the obstacles it faces both at home and abroad are formidable, and time is running out for the company — which generated only 4% of its 1998 revenues from international operations — to find the large telecom partner it so desperately needs to compete globally. Deutsche Telekom's trouble-plagued alliance with France Telecom and Sprint to provide worldwide services through Global One was recently put to rest in the form of a $4.3 billion buyout by

France Telecom. On the home front, Deutsche Telekom's core long-distance business has been fast eroding at the hands of aggressive new competitors like Mannesmann. Nonetheless, the carrier has successfully cut costs and generated growth in its Internet and mobile businesses. And through a $20 billion stock offering in June 1999, it is hoping to take its business to the next level.

➤ *British Telecommunications.* This U.K. carrier is also attempting to beat a strong global pathway for its long-distance and wireless businesses. British Telecom's fast-growing partnership with AT&T, aimed at building a global venture to serve the needs of businesses and individuals around the world (with anticipated first-year revenues in excess of $10 billion), is a major element in that strategy. Recent acquisitions and investments have included stakes in phone companies in Japan, Singapore, Hong Kong, Malaysia, and India. At home, BT recently placed a large order with France's Alcatel for ADSL equipment to strengthen its network technology.

■ THE NICHE PLAYERS

In today's tumultuous world of communications, however, size and heft are not always the answer. There is plenty of room for the so-called niche or specialized players who use their speed and agility to seek out specific geographies, markets, or applications. You might compare it to the airline industry, where under the nose of the major carriers like United and TWA smaller niche players like Southwest Airlines and USAir have carved out highly successful businesses.

By my estimates, there will be some 30 to 50 specialty telecom companies that can truly be called winners, though many more players will be competing. I've grouped these companies into three categories: geographic players, wholesalers, and resellers.

➤ Geographic Players

This group includes companies like Alltel, a fixed-line communications carrier serving over seven million customers in 23 states. This firm is also one of the largest wireless players in the U.S. with service coverage in rings around major metropolises. Led by the very able Jack Ford, Alltel is working under the radar screen of the big players like AT&T and Sprint, focusing on serving high-end businesses and residential customers in second- and third-tier cities.

When I think of successful specialty carriers, I also think of companies like SunCom, a wireless carrier that is pursuing a geographic niche strategy not unlike that of Alltel. For its part, SunCom is fixed on the East Coast beltway south of Philadelphia. The company's unique positioning also benefits AT&T, which owns a stake in SunCom and uses carrier's geographic reach to fill out its own wireless backbone.

➤ The Wholesalers

In addition to fixed wireline and wireless, the specialized carriers also include wholesalers. As the name suggests, these are companies that sell all or part of their services to other communications companies in areas where they need support. Williams Communications Companies, for instance, has an agreement with SBC Communications to supply network services to the RBOC on a national basis. SunCom not only maintains its own accounts, but serves as a wholesale provider of wireless to AT&T. There are clearly advantages today to using your network as a major opportunity for growth, not only via direct accounts, but through other telecom companies who desperately need what you have to offer.

➤ The Resellers

No discussion about specialty players is complete, however, without resellers, that fast-growing industry subset whose practitioners repackage and resell the services and products of others. Reselling can range from tiny start-ups that telemarket calling cards and long-distance service to megadeals that involve an industry giant like Time Warner serving as essentially a reseller of AT&T telephone service over its cable network.

It is certain that resellers will continue to play a key role in redefining the communications marketplace. That's because they are opening up vital new marketing and sales distribution channels for the traditional communications providers, ensuring them broader customer reach. Among the most successful resellers will be those that can bundle a range of services, especially value-added services, in a way that provides a one-stop shopping resource for customers.

■ REDEFINING THE PLAYING FIELD

As companies of all sizes and specialties are learning, communications is no longer a predictable, single-service industry where regulators have everyone marching in lockstep. The industry and the rules by which it plays are changing dramatically and, in the future, companies will be defined and their successes measured in ways that reflect not so much their technologies as their approaches to the marketplace.

No better example exists than the new breed of competitors helping redefine the industry through inventive niche strategies in areas as diverse as long distance, Internet access, and satellite communications. These newcomers are not only setting new market, service, and technical standards, but putting pressure on the established players to keep pace with the whirlwind changes that are breaking all around them.

Dismantling the Bell Dynasty

Here's a chronology of events behind one of the greatest breakups in corporate history:

1956—The U.S. Justice Department's Antitrust Division tries to get AT&T to divest Western Electric, its manufacturing arm. AT&T fights back, agreeing to not enter the computer business in return for keeping Western Electric.

1968—The Carterphone court decision holds that customers can plug in whatever equipment they want to the AT&T switched network. This decision is appealed, but upheld. AT&T required manufacturers of phone equipment other than Western Electric to buy PCAs (private coupling arrangements) for each piece of equipment connected to the AT&T network. Competing manufacturers resented this move, which was prominently featured in subsequent lawsuits as an example of AT&T's anticompetitiveness.

1969—MCI (Microwave Communications Inc.) gets regulatory approval to enter intercity private line business (using microwave towers) between Chicago and St. Louis. MCI promises lower rates than AT&T.

1973—MCI secures FCC permission to sell FX lines, allowing transfer of calls from one city to another via the use of local lines.

The Essential Facilities doctrine is enforced by the FCC. This states that if a company exclusively owns facilities that are essential to the business of another company, then the first company is required to provide access to the second company. The doctrine forces AT&T to allow MCI access to its local lines (the Bell System) to complete calls at a reasonable price. AT&T responds by requiring MCI to deal with each of the 22 Bell operating companies and 50 state public utility commissions.

1974—The U.S. Department of Justice, Antitrust Division, files a lawsuit against AT&T to break off Western Electric. AT&T protests that the case should be heard by the FCC, not by the courts.

1975—The case is put on hold for three years in order to resolve the dispute.

MCI begins Execunet service, connecting two FX (foreign exchange) lines, essentially providing long-distance service.

1976–1980—Various bills are presented to Congress to encourage competition within the nation's telephone system. All are defeated or passed to committees and die, some because of intense lobbying by AT&T.

1980 (June)—MCI's lawsuit against AT&T is decided, with AT&T ordered to pay MCI $1.8 billion. The annual interest alone is $162 million, more than MCI's 1979 revenue. Several years later, AT&T gets this judgment reduced on appeal.

1980 (December)—The Antitrust Division tries to settle its lawsuit against the telephone giant, proposing that AT&T spin off three of its operating companies (Pacific Bell, Southern New England Bell, and Cincinnati Bell) and 40% of Western Electric, and allow competitors access to its system. New lawyers enter the battle before the settlement can be finalized, however, and they request a postponement until they are more familiar with the case. Consequently, nothing is done to approve the settlement.

1981—Various Reagan administration cabinet members from departments other than Justice try to force a dismissal of the case. That effort dies, however, due to a combination of political and public relations issues.

1982—Charles Brown, chairman of AT&T, proposes a settlement to spin off the 22 Bell operating companies—the heart of the Bell Telephone System—while retaining all of Bell Labs and Western Electric. Under this settlement, AT&T would retain ownership of all phones in place, the Yellow Pages, production of phone equipment, and long-distance service. AT&T would also be able to enter the personal computer market.

1984—The settlement is finally approved with various modifications, including allowing the operating companies to produce the Yellow Pages.

The Logic behind the Breakup

The Justice Department was unhappy about the 1956 agreement to allow AT&T to retain Western Electric in return for not entering the computer market. It believed that AT&T, as a regulated business, should not be able to confer monopoly supply contracts on an unregulated business, Western Electric. Instead, the Justice Department felt Western Electric should be a separate entity and compete with other suppliers for the telephones and sundry equipment attached to the phone system.

The Antitrust Division pushed the idea of a 40% spin-off of Western Electric, embracing the company's telephone equipment manufacturing. This would have allowed AT&T to enter the computer business through Western Electric's manufacturing facilities. While AT&T publicly went along with the 40% spin-off, it was really opposed to divesting any part of Western Electric. However, it desperately wanted the 1956 restrictions on entering the computer marketplace lifted.

Antitrust Division lawyers were pushing for three Bell Operating Companies to be spun off as part of a settlement of the lawsuit against AT&T, while the Department of Defense wanted the suit dismissed altogether following AT&T's warning that a spin-off would jeopardize the Emergency Defense Telephone Network. At the same time, AT&T Chairman Brown raised eyebrows by proposing a settlement that included spinning off *all* of the operating companies. His rationale was that AT&T would have to make a major sacrifice to get the lawsuit dropped (the company was already on the defensive at the antitrust trial then in progress) and that losing the operating companies was preferable to losing even part of Western Electric. Brown was also eager to be allowed entry into the personal computer market, from which AT&T had been barred by the 1956 agreement with the Justice Department.

The Final Settlement

Under the terms of the final settlement, the 22 Bell Operating Companies were spun off into seven Regional Bell Operating Companies (RBOCs), each about equal in terms of assets and access lines. Moreover, each RBOC was large enough to attract capital and spread regulatory risk. None was considered large enough to retrigger the "size and power" antitrust issue.

The seven RBOCs and their components were:

➤ *Pacific Telesis* — Pacific Bell and Nevada Bell

➤ *U S WEST* — Mountain Bell, Northwestern Bell, Pacific Northwest Bell

➤ *Southwestern Bell Corporation* — Southwestern Bell

➤ *BellSouth* — South Central Bell, Southern Bell

➤ *Ameritech* — Illinois Bell, Indiana Bell, Michigan Bell, Ohio Bell, Wisconsin Telephone

➤ *Bell Atlantic* — Bell of Pennsylvania, Diamond State Telephone, The Chesapeake and Potomac Companies, New Jersey Bell

➤ *NYNEX* — New England Telephone, New York Telephone

The RBOCs had exclusive rights to the Bell name, though four chose not to use it. Their core business was to provide exchange service to customers and exchange access to long-distance companies so they could complete their calls to end customers. They were not allowed to manufacture equipment, set up exclusive equipment contracts with any one company, or discriminate against any long-distance company or equipment manufacturer. They did have the right to publish directories and provide electronic information services, including billing management, data transmission, address translation, protocol conversion, and introductory information content.

Under the terms of the final settlement, the RBOCs couldn't be acquired by corporations engaged in telecommunications activities that the BOCs couldn't perform themselves — primarily equipment manufacturing and providing long-distance service. After 1990, if specific conditions were met (primarily the opening of their local phone service markets to competition), the RBOCs (on an individual basis) would be allowed to enter the long-distance market.

AT&T was also free to enter the personal computer market under the settlement with the Justice Department, and did so in spring of 1984, just months after the settlement. AT&T's goal was to make UNIX the industry standard operating system, providing the vehicle for users to link together their personal computers with minis and mainframes.

Since the government had ruled that AT&T had to separate competitive equipment sales from regulated long-distance operations, the parts of Western Electric that made telephone equipment became AT&T Network Systems, while the long-distance operations became AT&T Communications. AT&T Information Systems was established to sell the PBX equipment used by larger companies. AT&T was precluded from purchasing stock and/or taking an ownership position in any of the RBOCs. The latter were free to purchase equipment from any company they chose.

Chapter

The Demolition-
Rebuilding Process

There's no denying the technical wizardry behind the explosion of communication applications transforming our lives. Revved-up, gigabit-speed networks and wireless devices that deliver the Internet in the palm of your hand are fueling the digital revolution. But there's another seismic force at work here. It's the restructuring—the virtual demolition and subsequent rebuilding—of an entire industry. And the catalyst for *that* change is not so much technology as the blitzkrieg of acquisitions, alliances, and mergers that's occurring, some of them with price tags that rival the GNPs of industrially developed nations.

To understand the dynamics of this giant work in progress is to recognize the true potential of the communications juggernaut, both now and in the year 2005. In the interest of clarity, I've broken the development process into five distinct and chronological building blocks. They begin with the most basic consolidation of local and long-distance voice communications, and proceed to the merger of cable TV and telephony, an unfolding movement that's being spearheaded by AT&T. Next on the timeline is the integration of diverse networks under a single corporate roof, a nascent drive that's triggering some of the largest acquisitions and mergers ever seen in the corporate firmament. With the foundation for the future firmly in place through the first three building blocks, the next step is providing structure through major alliances between large content and conduit providers. Finally, the integration of computing and communications is the capstone to everything that's come before. Designed to make information the centerpiece of our lives, it will be driven in the years ahead by alliances between technology and communications partners.

Here's a closer look at each of the five building blocks and how they're working to irrevocably reshape the industry.

■ BUILDING BLOCK 1: VOICE CONSOLIDATION

In the not-so-distant telecom past, there were local exchange and long-distance telephone companies, and there was no confusing the two. That structure is all but dead. That's because the new communications entities being built from the outcropping of acquisitions and mergers are set to provide both local and long-distance service via a single network that's transparent to the user. The goal behind these consolidations: provide participants with the footprint, technical heft, and critical mass they so urgently need to compete on telephone turf no longer circumscribed by local and long-distance boundaries.

Through this process of bulking up, SBC Communications, for example, hopes to counter the competitive threat posed by giants like AT&T and MCI WorldCom who, according to industry analysts, could siphon off 25% of SBC's local phone business by 2003, including some of its most lucrative business accounts. SBC has skillfully used acquisitions as a tool to extend its own footprint. If it needed an encore to its purchase of Pacific Telesis Group in 1997 and Southern New England Telephone Company in 1998, it did just that in 1999 with its $72 billion acquisition of Ameritech Corporation. This move created the nation's largest local telephone company with 55 million lines in 13 states, stretching from Michigan to Texas and also taking in Connecticut and California. The acquisition also increased SBC's heft in North America by adding Ameritech's slice of Bell Canada to its current stake in Telefonos de Mexico.

Within the United States, the Telecommunications Act of 1996 has intensified (some would say touched off) the acquisition-merger mania by establishing the ground rules under which local and long-distance players are allowed entry to each other's turf. Globally, the World Trade Organization (WTO) Telecommunications Agreement of 1997, signed by 72 member nations, has precipitated a similar chessboard-like game among the telecom players, with the largest using their size and power to penetrate countries once controlled by a single service provider.

Deutsche Telekom and British Telecom, for example, have become particularly active as they look for strong global positioning through strategic acquisitions. Their moves have bred both success and failure. Witness Deutsche Telekom's attempt to acquire Telecom Italia, the world's tenth-largest wireline communications company. In a highly publicized battle, the German carrier was beaten out by Italy-based Olivetti SpA, which engineered the first hostile takeover of a major European telecommunications firm and the largest such takeover ($64 billion) ever in Europe.

In the course of this global restructuring of telecommunications services, several models have emerged, though not all have proven to be built for success. In January 1996, Deutsche Telekom and France Telecom bought $3 billion of new preferred stock in Sprint for a 20% share of the company. From that deal was born Global One, a new company that tied together the voice and data networks of all three carriers to actively pursue customers whose communication needs stretched across countries and continents. But the alliance soon began to falter, plagued by an ineffective management structure, tension and feud-

World Trade Organization Agreement of 1997

On February 15, 1997, a new communications era dawned for much of the world. On that day 69 countries signed the first global pact on the deregulation of basic telecommunications markets at the World Trade Organization (WTO) conference in Geneva. This sweeping agreement opened the doors to competition across a wide range of telecommunications services, including voice telephony, fax, data transmission, cable, fiber optics, telex, telegraph, private communications, and cellular and mobile satellite services.

Specifically, signatories agreed to:

➤ Open their telecom markets to nondomestic operators.

➤ Liberalize foreign ownership regulations.

➤ Open their markets to additional satellite services.

The global telecommunications accord—which is expected to produce significant savings for consumers—was struck following nearly three years of negotiations. It opens up to competition not only the traditional telephony sector, but electronic data transmission (voice, images, and sound), and telex and fax services via all means of transmission, including cable, fiber optics, and satellite. The

ing among partners and, perhaps inevitably, consistent failure to return a profit. France Telecom mercifully put an end to the alliance with the recent buyout of its partners' shares for $4.3 billion.

What happened to a relationship that was conceived amid such great hopes and expectations? I believe one of the root problems was the creation of a separate operating entity—Global One—to provide a set of international communications services that essentially paralleled what the parent companies were already providing to their own cus-

agreement also establishes ground rules for telecommunications companies seeking to invest in other countries. Telecom industry giants like AT&T are free to request licenses to operate in Europe, just as major European companies are able to assume a stake in Asian telecom companies. The United States, led by Acting Trade Representative Charlene Barshefsky, pushed hard for the WTO agreement. U.S. companies can now compete on the world stage for local, long-distance, and international service either through resale or through their own facilities.

The WTO pact is the newest multinational agreement governing telecommunications, and the first to focus on basic services. It is actually part of a broader accord called the General Agreement on Trade in Services (GATS), which was negotiated during the Uruguay round of the General Agreement on Tariffs and Trade (GATT). The WTO pact also complements the Information Technology Agreement (signed two months earlier), designed to open global markets to telecommunications, telephone equipment, and other technology products.

The global agreement is expected to accelerate the trend toward greater market access, competition, and deregulation. It is also expected to create exciting new opportunities for telecom operators and equipment vendors worldwide. All told, 32 markets representing a staggering 90 percent of global telecom service revenues were opened following the signing of the historic WTO accord.

tomers. Factor in the fast-disappearing borders that have traditionally separated markets globally and the loss of market share by some of the alliance partners, and you clearly have a relationship headed for the rocks. Indeed, I believe Global One came to be seen by its founders as more of an encroachment than an adjunct to their respective businesses, and that resulted in an undertow of rivalry and division that never allowed the fledgling unit to get off the ground.

Other alliance models are emerging, however, that may

provide a more flexible platform for enabling partners to expand their market reach. Here the focus is not so much on creating a separate operating unit that might be perceived as a competitor as it is on integrating the partners' networks along with their sales and marketing resources to provide a seamless, universal service for customers. AT&T appears to be pursuing that strategic pathway in its alliance with British Telecom. To give their customers consistent technology and support anywhere in the world, the partnership combines AT&T's and BT's international operations, network assets, and customer relationships. Together, the telecom giants are designing a common network architecture to link the world's leading 100 economic centers at 200 gigabits per second (the equivalent of a single fiber carrying 2.6 million calls simultaneously). Defining this network for the transmission of voice, data, video, and Internet services is the Internet protocol standard. AT&T decided to further support the alliance through its $5 billion acquisition of IBM's global network, a facility that serves thousands of businesses and more than one million individual Internet users in 59 countries. Enriching that blossoming alliance is the linkage of AT&T's and BT's wireless telephone operations to serve some 41 million customers in 17 countries.

Another global powerhouse in the wireless field was created when Britain's Vodafone Group snatched AirTouch Communications from the embrace of Bell Atlantic in a two-week bidding war that Vodafone won in summer 1999 with a $60 billion offer. In the process, Vodafone boosted its subscriber base from 10.4 million to more than 29 million wireless customers across four continents. Nine months later, Vodafone stunned the communications world by signing a deal with its erstwhile adversary Bell Atlantic, to combine their U.S. cellular operations to create the nation's largest wireless network. The new joint venture company now called Verizon Communications, with over 23 million subscribers, is designed to give both companies the scale they needed to compete against AT&T and SBC.

■ BUILDING BLOCK 2: CABLE-TELEPHONY CONSOLIDATION

Cable television networks possess what the copper wire telephone companies feverishly wish they had: broadband capabilities. For that reason, cable, which snakes into two-thirds of all U.S. homes, is being adopted and positioned by a segment of the telecommunications industry as the lead vehicle for delivering the long-promised trove of digital communications services to the public. And as that happens, voice and entertainment will become virtually indistinguishable as they travel as bits over the same cable network.

AT&T is leading the charge here, having acquired cable giants Tele-Communications, Inc. (TCI) for $55 billion and MediaOne for $58 billion to become the nation's largest cable company, with access to 26% of the homes in the United States. These acquisitions will enable AT&T to bundle over its new broadband property such services as local and long-distance telephone, cable television, and Internet access. At the same time, they will enable AT&T to use its cable lines to compete aggressively with the Regional Bell Operating Companies for local telephone service as it seeks to break the RBOCs' dominance of the $110 billion market.

The movement to merge cable and telephony is well under way. And while it is making headway primarily through acquisitions, strategic alliances are also a part of the equation. Witness the joint venture between AT&T and Time Warner, one of the largest cable operators, to offer local telephone service over the latter's cable network.

■ BUILDING BLOCK 3: NETWORK INTEGRATION

The consolidation of communications companies is leading inexorably to the integration of networks. Companies that have historically managed a single network technology, like fixed wireline, are now finding that they must be able to manipulate multiple technologies — including wireless, satellite, and cable — if they are to deliver the mélange of services that customers are starting to demand, from voice, data, and Internet access to video and multimedia. Even more important, they must have the ability to manage their network and its components in a way that is totally transparent to the customer. The business traveler in Morocco simply doesn't care if his or her call is routed via satellite or transatlantic cable. They just want a fast and flawless connection.

Because network integration is so critical to the provider's ability to offer bundled services to customers, the third building block stands as the beacon for much of the consolidation that's taking place in the industry today. When MCI WorldCom ponied up $129 billion for Sprint Corporation in what at the time was the largest merger ever attempted, it had Sprint PCS, the company's high-flying wireless business, in its crosshairs. By plugging a long-standing hole in MCI WorldCom's network fortress, Sprint PCS, with its exceptional voice and data transfer capabilities, would have put the new enterprise closer to its goal of becoming the preeminent supplier of long-distance, data, and wireless services to corporate customers. For now, MCI WorldCom remains without its own wireless network.

SBC Communications is also mending a network vulnerability through its merger with BellSouth's wireless division. SBC has forged a relationship with DirectTV Inc., the nation's largest direct broadcast satellite provider. This marketing and distribution agreement is enabling SBC to weave television programming into its network fabric, drawing the company closer to its avowed goal of offering an integrated, one-stop shopping experience for customers that includes local and long distance, wireless, video, and Internet access—all on a single bill.

■ BUILDING BLOCK 4: CONTENT VERSUS CONDUIT

Here's where the rubber begins to meet the road. With building blocks one, two, and three providing the structural foundation for an adventuresome new communications era, the next two building blocks offer concrete evidence of how our lives will be directly affected. Building block four is being shaped by the face-off between content (digital information, including voice, data, video, or multimedia) and conduit (the process for distributing this information to the network user). The debate revolves around this overarching question: Will the industry evolve so that the major players provide both content and conduit, or will separate companies provide these two fundamental services?

On one side of the issue are companies that are content rich, but have some distribution capabilities. They include Walt Disney, whose empire consists of TV studios, films, publishing, cable holdings (including The Disney Channel and ESPN) and the ABC Network; and Viacom, which embraces Hollywood studios, cable properties (including MTV, Nickelodeon, and The Nashville Network), radio stations, and the CBS Network. Time Warner is cut from the same cloth, integrating its publishing empire with its TV production and popular cable networks, including CNN and HBO. AOL Time Warner will add an Internet services capability to this powerful media mix.

On the other side of the content-conduit issue are companies who act principally as purveyors of distribution services. They include the leading communications service providers like SBC, Qwest, MCI WorldCom, and AT&T.

In the past, these companies have been loath to get involved in content.

Indeed, the bulk of activity to date has revolved around companies rich in content deciding they need a guaranteed distribution channel to relay that information and programming to their customers. That rationale, I believe, prompted Walt Disney to acquire the ABC Network and Viacom to purchase the CBS Network. But in terms of how the building blocks will eventually fit together, I see the major TV networks — ABC, CBS, and NBC — as interim solutions or bridges that will get their parent companies to the next, and more crucial, stage of development. What, really, is the advantage of Walt Disney or Viacom having a television network that is one-way and highly constrained in the programming it can deliver to consumers?

That's the question I'm sure that Walt Disney and Viacom are already asking themselves. The answer from the distribution companies would be unequivocal. Viacom would learn from MCI WorldCom, for example, that instead of having to settle for a single channel (i.e., CBS) it could secure 12 channels on the carrier's global wideband network to provide the kinds of flexible, interactive programming, web access, and multimedia capabilities it could never hope to achieve on its own. It's intriguing to ponder the possibilities: dedicated Viacom channels for kids, teens, recent movies, interactive games, home shopping, downloadable consumer/business applications, personalized news and features, and much more, all accessible when and where the user wants them from TV screens, computers, or hand-held devices. CBS, acquired by Viacom in 1999, might retain its name, but it would in all likelihood wind up a single all-news/information channel on Viacom's diverse programming lineup.

Driving the industry purposefully in this direction will be a new wave of strategic alliances between the large content and conduit providers. The AOL Time Warner deal has injected a new note of urgency into the mating game. Joining the party, in addition to all the aforementioned players, are strong web portal companies like Yahoo!, Oracle, and Microsoft. And while any alliances these companies may forge will dramatically alter the world of content-conduit, I believe that for the biggest winners in the twenty-first century they will merely serve as an entree to the final and most important building block within our industry structure—computing-communications integration.

■ BUILDING BLOCK 5: COMPUTING-COMMUNICATIONS INTEGRATION

This clearly has the potential to be the boldest and most exciting stroke of the communications work in progress. Indeed, the linkage of computing and network technologies promises to put information at the fingertips of people in an outpouring of new and exciting ways. As a consumer, I'll have a chance to program all the things that are important to my life so I have greater flexibility, greater resources, greater control than ever before. Picture this scenario:

> *I learn via an early morning message from the airline that my 9 A.M. flight is stuck on the ground and that I've been rescheduled for 10:30. This gives me an unexpected hour-and-a-half windfall. I use the time productively, accessing an auto locator service through my WebTV (compliments of the ever-widening partnership between computing and communications) to find the best deal on a Chevy Blazer I've had my eye on, along with the best financing rates from over 500 institutions. This information alone saves me days of work—and aggravation.*
>
> *As I relax with a second cup of coffee, my eyes remain glued to the TV screen in front of me. My communications carrier has put at my fingertips over 200 channels of programming and information. I stop briefly at the sports scores from the previous evening,*

then move on to a preprogrammed summary of busi-
ness news that's of interest to me, and finally switch to
my own personal channel. This posts my hour-by-hour
schedule for the day (it's been conveniently updated
and forwarded by my associate at work); today it also
offers a clip from that morning's Wall Street Journal,
which my company's librarian has thoughtfully posted
for me, knowing it contains some information I can use
in a presentation I'm giving later in the day.

Before powering down my system, I dial directly
into my airline's departure schedule for that morning
to review the status of my flight. I'm relieved to see that
my second cup of coffee won't be turning into a third,
or a fourth.

In sum, the integration of computing and networks will
pave the way for a whole new generation of interactive services allowing users to obtain, manipulate, and synthesize
data to meet their specific information needs. Positioned
squarely behind this sea change will be what I call the
thinking network — a network that will soar to new heights
of sophistication with the help of advanced software systems. It will open the door, for example, to multimedia
applications that marry voice, full-motion video, and
graphics in ways that engage all our senses. It will make it
possible — through vital business support systems downloaded from the Net — to set up a new enterprise in a matter
of hours or days, instead of weeks or months, and at a frac-
tion of the traditional cost.

Who the major players will be in this pivotal computing-communications space is still unclear. What *is* clear,
however, is that strategic alliances will again provide the
requisite spark. Foreshadowing this movement is AT&T's
alliance with Microsoft. In return for its $5 billion invest-
ment in AT&T, Microsoft is assured that its Windows CE
operating system will power millions of digital set-top
boxes — the home-based command centers — in AT&T's
growing cable television universe.

The concept of computers and networks converging is itself an example of a macroalliance between two unlikely partners: Silicon Valley on the West Coast and the communications industry rooted on the East Coast. While they have typically been competitors in the past, it is a partnership that makes eminent sense in this new age of the intelligent network. If anybody can empower the network, it's Silicon Valley, whose practitioners have a long history of converting technical research into practical applications that allow people to do things cheaper, faster, better. This is something the communications industry hasn't shown itself nearly as adept at over the years.

Both industries have already responded to the challenge by working jointly to integrate public network with private network (local area network and wide area network) technologies. This integration has been accelerating within the industry as companies seek to combine the traditional benefits of private networks — particularly privacy, security, and unrestricted usage — with the extended reach and e-business opportunities of the Internet, including intranets and extranets. One solution has been the development of virtual private networks (VPNs), which combine the structure of the Internet with the security and reliability of private networks.

The bond between communications and computing will produce many more advanced services that will help to revolutionize the field of communications. It's no wonder that Lucent Technologies acquired Ascend Communications and has begun moving an army of key people to Silicon Valley to be where the action is, or that communications services are starting to be viewed by Silicon Valley as the next major development frontier, with abundant opportunity and money-making potential.

■ ALLIANCES POINT THE WAY

While acquisitions and mergers have carried the communications industry through its groundbreaking stages of transformation, it is strategic alliances that will provide a robust platform for the growth of its member companies over the next five years. The real ability to execute, to give people the access and advanced services they need to navigate in an information-intensive age, will depend on how well the key players can pool their talents, resources, and muscle. The task has become so big and complex that no company can hope to go it alone. But it's equally clear that no communications enterprise should undertake an alliance for the simple sake of a relationship. It should be done with the overriding goal of improving a company's weak points or building on its strengths to make it a more potent force in the marketplace.

As the old industry order continues to crumble, alliances and consolidation are providing the cohesion and scale for a powerful new structure to rise in its place. The public's increasing thirst for faster, better, cheaper communications will only add fuel to that collaborative process.

Chapter

Communications' Yellow Brick Road

Despite the pitched battles it has inspired, the last mile may not qualify as the most valuable stretch of telecom highway in the future. Equally likely to gain that distinction is what I have termed the extra mile, which begins at the front door and meanders throughout the home. Under the industry's new rules of the open road, this coveted space will no longer be dominated by telecommuters or other work-at-home types. It will become a *teleliving* quarters for all family members, offering untold opportunities for new applications and revenue growth by communications service providers.

It's not hard to imagine the stratospheric market potential awaiting any company that can effectively manage and link the deluge of digital devices that are starting to penetrate the home, from computing to entertainment to home maintenance and automation. Consider:

➤ PCs are starting to infiltrate nearly every room of the house (see Figure 3.1) and will desperately need a way to share Internet access. According to The Yankee Group, households with more than one PC are expected to grow to 24 million by 2001, and 90% of those machines will be online (see Figure 3.2). And it's not unreasonable to suggest that with the Inter-

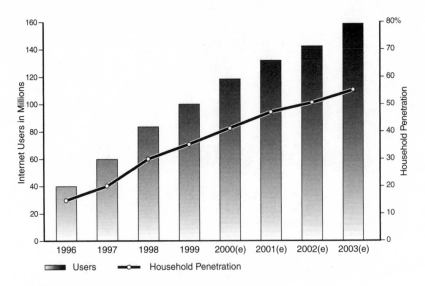

Figure 3.1 U.S. Households Online

Source: Jupiter Communications

net instantly available and always "on," family members will be riveted to web sites for local news and weather, movie listings, traffic reports, physician referrals, shopping bargains, and much more.

➤ WebTV and Internet-enabled screen phones in upward of 10 million U.S. homes by 2002 (according to *The Forrester Report*) will need connections for accessing e-mail, web surfing, and Internet phone services.

➤ Consumers of all ages will want to ride the latest technology wave of downloading music from the Internet and playing it back on home stereos, or running a DVD movie on a computer in the den, say, and displaying it on a large television screen in the living room. Other entertainment cognoscenti will want to access the web to ensure their home theater systems have the optimal surround-sound setting.

➤ Heating, electrical, and security systems will be connected to the web, allowing for an intriguing range

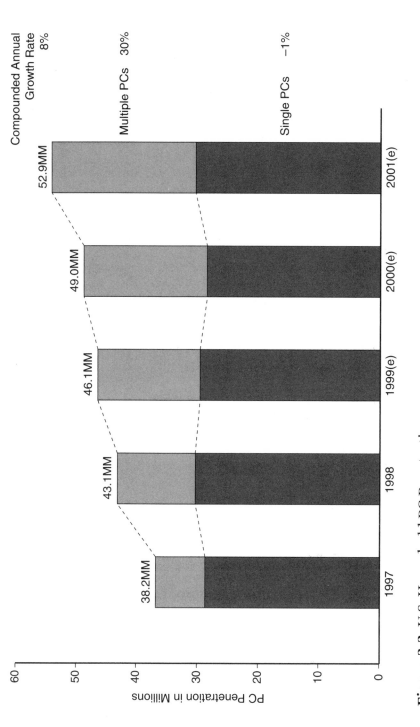

Figure 3.2 U.S. Household PC Penetration

Source: The Yankee Group

of home-based applications. Utility companies could offer consumers financial incentives in return for agreeing to peak-period adjustments, for example. By the same token, an individual could issue a command from a computer at work to turn down (or up) the thermostat at home, or arm the security system, or start cooking a casserole dinner that's sitting on the stove.

■ THE ENABLING HOME AREA NETWORK

The common thread through each of these applications is the emerging home area network. A scalable version of the local area networks that have for years connected computers and peripherals within the work setting, the home area network is destined to become the next market tsunami. By evolving into a home network hub, it will have the ability to offload network-specific tasks from smart devices like PCs while enabling dumb devices like VCRs and thermostats to access and interact with Internet-based applications. The possibilities are indeed tantalizing. Household members—each with their own computers and daily agendas—would be able to share not just high-speed Internet access but printers, scanners, and other peripherals. Through the ability to share files (one machine might be designated the central server) they could enhance communications and catch up on each other's schedules whether inside or outside the home.

As consumers become more and more aware of their advantages, home area networks could, according to some projections, penetrate 10% of all U.S. households by 2002 (see Figure 3.3). But it seems certain that much of that success will depend on how readily adaptable these devices are to the home environment. Actually, home area networks have been commercially available for some time in the form of kits priced at around $200 that typically connect

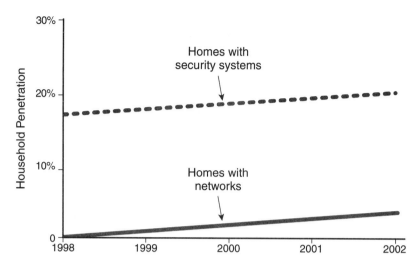

Figure 3.3 Penetration of Home Area Networks
Source: Forrester Research

via phone lines (or in some cases via electrical outlets or wireless connections) and require opening the computer case for PCI card installation.

Home area networks of the future will have to be virtual no-brainers if they are to reach their full potential—as plug-and-play or wireless devices no more difficult to install than today's telephones. 3Com already has a jump on the market through its HomeConnect products. Teaming up with Microsoft, 3Com is bringing out a line of easy-to-use Ethernet, phone line, or wireless home network kits, with a suite of home productivity, education, and entertainment applications on the way.

Where does this household high-tech leave the communications industry? Sitting in the catbird seat of opportunity. The home area network could be a significant product differentiator for service providers, who might resell the devices or bundle them as part of broad product/service/application offerings.

Home area networks—and, for that matter, the whole teleliving space—really make sense for communications service providers when they start looking on the last mile as their entree to not just the household, but individual members, each with distinct needs and predilections. This opens up a wide swath of opportunities aimed at the personal and business application needs of each member, and could even play off the relationships *between* family members. What do I mean by that? Let's say my local telephone company offers me video games for the kids over my cable (or DSL) lines. Okay, the price sounds right, but there's no way I'm going to subscribe to a service like this unless I can exercise strict control over the deliverables. That's where the telcos can play a critical value-added role, developing and providing a network-based application that allows me as a parent to carefully define what kinds of video games my kids play, and during what hours they can play them. Other telco-tailored applications might allow my kids to get or confirm their class assignments over the web, or enable my wife and me to indulge our passion for antiques by keeping track of any sales in our area. The list goes on and on.

The competition among communications companies for the extra-mile customer promises to be stiff. But the rewards will more than justify the effort for those players who can harness the teleliving space through market segmentation and individual tailoring of products and services.

■ A KLONDIKE OF OPPORTUNITY

For all its potential, the home area network is just the tip of the iceberg when it comes to uncovering major new revenue streams for resourceful businesses. Some other fertile fields include:

> ➤ *Enhanced network services.* Time was when *enhanced services* meant things like call waiting and call forwarding. With the growing sophistication of the net-

work, the term now refers to a whole new set of advanced features that providers can offer. Enhanced network services can range from network security monitoring to automated billing information to message consolidation. The last consists of services that simplify things for customers by enabling them to consolidate and retrieve all their messages—voice, e-mail, and fax—from a single collection site, in a single mode. Message consolidation is being actively pursued by companies like OneBox, which gives each subscriber a telephone number that they in turn give to any individual who wants to leave a voice, fax, or e-mail message. (The downside is that this service is not terribly secure.) Other companies are starting to jump on this enhanced network service bandwagon.

➤ *Customer outsourcing services.* As customers focus on developing and maintaining their core competencies, they will continue to outsource those functions that third parties can do better and cheaper. This is spawning an entire new industry of application service providers (ASPs) who are designing and implementing for clients Internet-based solutions that can search for information, develop trend analyses, summarize results, handle scheduling, facilitate interactive communications, improve productivity, and more.

My previous company is helping to spearhead this movement. As an application service provider, KPMG has teamed up with Qwest Communications to offer middle-market companies an efficient new way to run their businesses. Instead of continuing to rely on complex internal systems, these companies can now access applications like Oracle, SAP, and PeopleSoft through the Internet. By outsourcing their vital applications, they're not only relieved of a huge upfront hardware/software expense, but they're able to offload technical issues and problems onto the shoulders of the experts at KPMG and Qwest. Oracle has itself become an ASP. Oracle Business OnLine gives clients access to a suite of business applications through their web browsers for a monthly fee based on usage.

➤ *Enhanced information services.* Services with the ability to search a multitude of sources on the Net for specific information and summarize the results for customers will grow rapidly on an information-hungry public. There's no overestimating the demand for service providers who could, for example, find the cheapest mortgage rate in the region or the best deal on a Ford Escort. Communications service providers might tap into this opportunity by becoming "portals of the future." Instead of logging onto Yahoo!, for example, customers would access AT&T or their local exchange carrier, who would go out and get for them the desired information.

Directory services are another example of this new breed of information portal. Providers with experience in the directory field will have a unique opportunity to package and deliver online or via the telephone sundry types of information in response to consumer requests—like the closest board-certified cardiologist, or a four-star Portuguese restaurant in a neighboring city, or a local contractor who specializes in gazebos.

Other enhanced information services might include consolidated billing with the capacity to separate company and private calls for business customers, and online community information services in such areas as children's vaccination schedules, shopping updates, and local and state government services.

➤ *Transaction services.* The ubiquity of the Net has touched off a revolution in the way consumers shop, bank, look for jobs, handle their investments, and, increasingly, manage their daily lives. The pacesetters when it comes to providing the enabling online connection are companies like Amazon.com, the web's leading retail store; eBay, the largest person-to-person auction web site; and E*Trade and Charles Schwab & Co., who, virtually overnight, redefined the world of commercial brokerage services. Opportunities exist for scores of other firms that can harness the energy of the Internet to handle endless types of transactions. Think of enterprising ventures like PriceLine.com, which allows consumers to name their price for airline tickets, hotel accommodations, groceries, and more. How about automated shopping services that are making their presence known on the Net? These "robotic" shoppers, or bots, not only search out the best deals for buyers, but have the authorization to make the purchase if the price and features are right.

Clearly, the opportunities are endless when it comes to harnessing the power of the network, but the competition will be ferocious. The winners will be those companies that are the most determined and, without doubt, the most inventive. And as I see it, that doesn't mean being the most technologically astute. What it does mean is being the most market savvy–knowing what the public wants and how to position that need on the extraordinarily broad shoulders of the Internet.

Chapter 4

Who Needs All That Capacity?

Since 1965, Moore's law has served as a bedrock principle for the computer industry. That law, first stated by Gordon Moore, a cofounder of Intel Corporation, holds that every 18 months the processing power of computer chips will double while costs hold constant (see Figure 4.1). Over the years, Moore's law has been amazingly accurate, prefiguring not just the exponential increase in computing power but the plummeting price of personal computers from thousands to hundreds of dollars today.

While Moore's law has been critical in addressing the pure issue of chip capacity, it stopped short of responding to an equally important economic corollary: If processing speeds double every 18 months, will there actually be a marketplace demand for that pyramiding capacity?

I've attempted to answer that question as it relates to the communications industry by developing a comparable law. There are, to be sure, many parallels between the computing and communications industries. Communications networks, for example, run on routers, which are switch-like components resembling computers. Thus, the speed of routers is analogous to the speed of processors. The major difference between the computing and communications industries is that capacity in the latter is measured in terms of bandwidth. And significantly, *that*

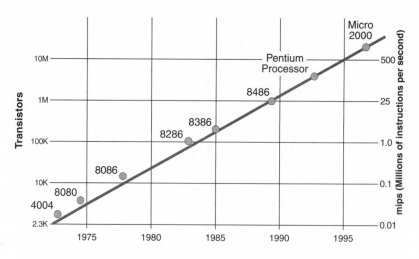

Figure 4.1 Moore's Law of Chip Performance Progression
Source: Intel Corporation

capacity is increasing at an even faster rate than Moore's law describes.

Why is that so? Primarily because the increased processing speeds of routers are augmented by improved methods of compressing signals—particularly dense wavelength division multiplexing (DWDM)—in the fiber that carries voice and data signals. All told, innovations from Lucent Technologies, Cisco Systems, and Nortel Networks have tremendously increased the data capacity of each strand of fiber.

The combination of Moore's law, DWDM, and other technological improvements has provided the foundation for a bandwidth law that has proven extremely reliable to date: The amount of data that can be moved over a single strand of fiber doubles every 12 months.

As advances in the transmission of voice and data occur, it is reasonable to conclude that bandwidth capacity will continue its sharp ascent. Accelerating the growth curve will be new technologies, like digital subscriber line (DSL), satellite, and other forms of wireless, which add significant broadband capabilities.

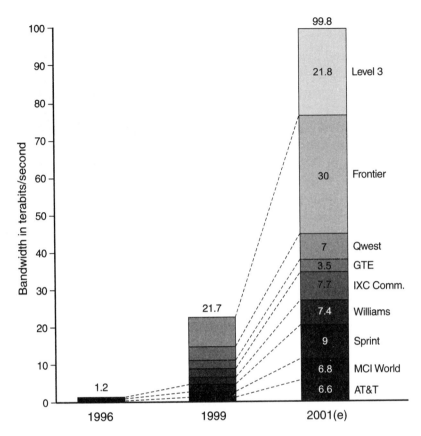

Figure 4.2 U.S. Communications Bandwidth Supply

Source: Fortune

Predictably, this track record has led to concerns — particularly within the investment community — that bandwidth has become not only a commodity, but a commodity flush with excess capacity. Consider the projection from *Fortune* that the national long-haul telecommunications infrastructure will, by 2001, boast more than 80 times the capacity present in 1996 (see Figure 4.2).

What does this say, then, about the pricing and profitability outlook for communications companies with huge fixed infrastructure assets? The prognosis might be gloomy if capacity were the only factor being weighed. But in fact, the long-range prospects of the communication sector are impacted by more than how much data can be compressed into a strand of transmission fiber. Cost, price, and demand are pivotal issues. It's a simple economic principle that reductions in cost and price will stimulate demand for data transmission.

I've tried to take these various factors into account in coming up with a new guiding principle for the industry that goes beyond the Moorean issue of capacity only. By looking at other key factors impacting the growth of communications, it attempts to quantify actual demand for emerging services. With all due respect to Mr. Moore, I refer to this new principle as Bonocore's hypothesis: For every 1% decrease in the price of bandwidth, there will be an accompanying 3% increase in the demand for network capacity.

How did I arrive at this marketplace principle, which essentially holds that demand will expand sufficiently to fill virtually all available bandwidth? Here's the thinking behind Bonocore's hypothesis.

■ THE ISSUE OF COST

There is good reason to expect considerable cost reductions going forward for communications capacity. For one thing, technological improvements in routers and fiber optics are resulting in rapid declines in the cost of transmitting data over networks. Routers, for example, are doubling their price-performance ratio every 20 months, and fiber optic cable and other technological advances are doubling the speed and capacity of network transmission every 10 months. New IP (Internet protocol) networks, which use packet switching to economically transmit digital information over high-speed fiber trunk lines, are also driving down the cost of transmission.

■ THE ISSUE OF PRICE

There are no guarantees that falling costs will produce commensurate declines in the price of bandwidth. But history strongly suggests that when the element of competition is introduced in virtually any field — particularly communications — there will be a tight linkage between cost and price.

Essentially, competition works to reduce prices by eroding the market power of dominant players. It also ensures that the preponderance of cost reductions will be passed on to consumers rather than to service providers in the form of higher profits. In both the communications equipment industry and the network infrastructure industry, competition has increased feverishly in recent years. In the equipment industry, Cisco Systems continues to dominate in the production of routers, with about 80 percent market share. But competition is intensifying from Lucent, Nortel, and European entries like Alcatel, Ericsson, and Siemens.

In terms of network infrastructure, a field that was dominated by AT&T, MCI WorldCom, and Sprint has broadened to include Qwest, Level 3, Global Crossing, IXC Communications, and the communications units of energy companies Williams and Enron. The net result of this escalating competition has been dramatic increases in available bandwidth and corresponding reductions in price. Similar price reductions have occurred in the wireless market where the advent of PCS technology has helped to fuel intense competition (see Figure 4.3).

Based on the bandwidth law (the amount of data that can be moved over a single strand of fiber doubles every 12 months) and the experience of network segments like wireless and T1/T3 lines that have been impacted by competition, I believe it is reasonable to expect the price of raw bandwidth to continue to decrease at 10% per year. But another element enters into the calculation: the price of *using* bandwidth. Most consumers do not purchase raw band-

Service	Time Period	Price Change or Difference	
T3 Line	1996–1999	–28%	○
T1 Line, Qwest vs. AT&T	1999	–41%	○
Wireless Telephone— Yankee Group wireless price index	1995–1998	–40%	○
Overall cost of bandwidth in large U.S. cities with significant competition	1994–1999	–90%	○

Figure 4.3 Price Reductions in Network Infrastructure
Source: Forrester Research

width. Instead, communications service providers use that raw bandwidth as the foundation for value-added services and applications that are offered to the public. Based on the experience of other industries that have deregulated, I believe the price of using bandwidth will decline to the tune of about 5% annually.

■ THE ISSUE OF DEMAND

There seems little doubt that price declines will combine with new and lower-cost ways of using bandwidth to stimulate unprecedented consumer demand. Indeed, falling prices will certainly stoke demand for a host of sophisticated new applications triggered by the Internet and the integration of computing and communications.

But does all this evidence conclusively prove Bonocore's hypothesis: that every 1% decrease in the price of bandwidth will generate a 3% increase in the demand for network capacity? There is no way to conclusively prove Bonocore's hypothesis—it's not a physical law. However, economic analysis supports its validity.

Service	Time Period	Elasticity
Cable Television	1990	−2.2
Purchase Wireless Telephone	1996 1997	−1.5 −0.7
Trucking (leather, rubber, plastic products)	1981	−2.97
Railroads (transport equipment)	1981	−2.68

Figure 4.4 Elasticity Measurements

Source: The Yankee Group

As previously discussed, the anticipated yearly doubling in the capacity of a strand of fiber for the next several years is likely to result in an annual price reduction of about 10% for overall raw bandwidth. On top of that, the price of using bandwidth for various value-added consumer applications is likely to decline by 5% annually, as measured against declines in other industries. How will consumers react to these price decreases? Economists measure the level of response in terms of the *price elasticity* of demand—that is, the percentage change in demand that results from a 1% decrease in price. In the communications market, an elasticity measure of −2.0 seems justified (see Figure 4.4). That is, for every 1% decline in price, there is a 2% increase in demand.

Extrapolating from that data, a 10% decrease in raw bandwidth prices each year will increase bandwidth demand by 20%. On top of that, the 5% decline in the price of using bandwidth increases demand by 10% (see Figure 4.5). Each year, then, the total increase in demand is 120% × 110% = 132% of the previous year. This translates into a 32% annual increase in demand for bandwidth given a 10% reduction in price, or a 3.2% increase in demand for each 1% decline in bandwidth price. In short, these calculations support Bonocore's hypothesis, which posits a 3:1 ratio of increased demand to decreased price.

Industry— Type of Estimate	Time Frame	Estimate
Wireless Telephone— Penetration vs. income in nine European cities	1999	Approx. 20% rise in penetration for a 2% decrease in the share of monthly income devoted to cellular
Cellular Telephone— Price elasticity of minutes of usage	1991–1995	−1.63
Purchase Telephone— Price elasticity of minutes of usage	1996 1997	−1.50 −0.69
Digital Cellular— Price elasticity of minutes of usage	1996 1997	−1.31 −1.24

Figure 4.5 Estimates of Demand Elasticity

Source: The Yankee Group

■ BUILD AWAY!

From this blizzard of numbers emerges a very encouraging bottom line for the communications industry: The public's insatiable demand for new applications ensures that the extraordinary capacity now being created will be fully utilized. In some cases, such as the demand for broadband Internet access, the application is actually well ahead of the technology (capacity) curve.

Bonocore's hypothesis serves to allay fears that service providers are creating a network of such vast proportions that even skyrocketing demand for Internet applications—including business-to-business and business-to-consumer, as well as other advanced data applications—could never be able to fill the pipe. The hypothesis offers concrete evidence that the massive infrastructure development under way rests on a solid foundation, and that there will indeed be demand for the robust, interactive market that's rapidly taking shape around computer-communications integration. As long as communications service providers continue to translate cost savings into price reductions—and as long as other integral factors like regulation, competition, and technology fall in to place—there is every reason to believe that customers will beat a wide path to their door.

Chapter

Policing the Communications Highway

In Montana, there is no speed limit. You want to do 120 miles per hour on the open highway, no one is going to stop you.

Following passage of the Telecommunications Act of 1996, many onlookers envisioned the communications industry as turning into a similar unchecked, unfettered roadway. In this new deregulated environment, long-distance carriers, local telephone providers, and cable companies would now have the ability to freely switch lanes—cruise right into each other's competitive space—without an official in sight to stop them.

To date, the Telecommunications Act hasn't begun to touch off the kind of competitive free-for-all that was originally envisioned. While the law has prompted many small carriers to enter the local services market and has helped to drive down long-distance and wireless prices, it has not yet significantly changed the competitive dynamics of the long-distance, local telephone, or even the cable industry. The long-awaited entry of the Baby Bells into long-distance, and of AT&T and a battery of new competitors into the local service arena, has developed at a snail's pace.

There are a number of reasons for this. One of the most obvious is that ambiguities in the law triggered a rash of lawsuits that has since stymied its implementation by the FCC. A more basic reason, however, is that real competition within the telecommunications industry will not take place until the major players have begun duking it out with each other on the fields of local and long-distance service. What happened in the first wave after the 1996 act was, predictably, the creation of many small carriers—the competitive local exchange companies (CLECs)—who began nibbling at the customer base of the big regional players. And while they have successfully captured a growing market share, it is, nonetheless, a very small share, one that which will not change appreciably until the entrenched local carriers start to feel the hot breath of industry heavyweights like AT&T and SBC-Ameritech on their necks. That is now starting to happen, and will intensify more than most people realize in the future.

Another reason why the Telecommunications Act has proven disappointing to many people, I believe, is that their definition of deregulation is substantially different from what the 1996 law had in mind. The dictionary defines *deregulation* as the removal of regulations or restrictions from an object. Most people took the new law in the most literal sense—the excision of all regulations. That was never the intent, however, of the Telecommunications Act. Instead of deregulation, a better term might be *demiregulation,* which roughly translates into continued constraints on parts of the business, even as regulatory controls are generally eased, or changed.

Which is the way it should be. The Telecommunications Act recognized the barriers that exist between the delivery of various forms of communication—voice, data, video—and sought to remove many of those impediments at a time of growing convergence within the industry. But in a host of other areas the government can indeed play a critical role in promoting competition and creating a strong industry model for the future by pushing for constructive change and flexible new ground rules. Those areas include universal service, open access, standardizing regulations within the industry, and accelerated research and development.

■ THE EARLY SIGNS OF CHANGE

There is no mistaking the movement to deregulate and privatize the communications services industry at local, national, and global levels. It has become well understood around the world that public control or ownership of communications companies has served to limit their ability to take necessary risks, make appropriate investments, and provide leading-edge services to their customers. Regulatory edicts that have set the stage for major changes in the way telecom services are managed and provided to customers include the Global Telecommunications Reform Act of 1997, and the U.S. Telecommunications Act of 1996.

Even with its obvious flaws, the U.S. act stands as a milestone for the industry, the first major overhaul of federal communications law since the FCC was created in 1934. In signing the legislation into law, President Clinton called it an important step in his administration's commitment to reform the telecommunications laws in a way that would lead to increased competition and private investment, promote universal service and open access to information networks, and provide for flexible government regulation.

At its core, the Telecommunications Act sought to bring about greater competition across various markets by taking steps to encourage new entrants into the telecom space. It did this by eliminating legal barriers to entry and, at the local competitive level, requiring incumbent local telephone companies to interconnect and exchange traffic with new entrants into the market on nondiscriminatory terms. The act also required the incumbent carriers to lease parts of their networks (like switches and customer lines)

The Telecommunications Act of 1996

In signing the Telecommunications Act of 1996, President Clinton set in motion the first major revisions to federal communications law in 62 years. The legislation was not really a new law but a substantial rewriting of the Communications Act of 1934. In 1979 a number of Congressional members launched efforts to update or replace that act, which after years of hard work and debate reached fruition in 1996 when the act was passed overwhelmingly by the House and Senate. The act clearly sets forth its goal: "To promote competition and reduce regulation in order to secure lower prices and higher quality services for American telecommunications consumers and encourage the rapid deployment of new telecommunications technologies."

The Telecommunications Act primarily affects local exchange carriers (LECs), interexchange carriers (IXCs), cable TV, and broadcasting. Under the new law, vendors in each of these industries may enter each other's markets. Additionally, the law impacts telecommunications resellers, competitive access providers (CAPs), Internet service providers (ISPs), value-added network providers, and a variety of other communications and network service vendors, all of whom are dependent upon the services of the LEC, IXC, cable TV, and broadcasting industries.

Key elements of the Telecommunications Act include:

Title I. Telecommunications Services

➤ Calls for establishment of a nondiscriminatory telecommunications market environment and requests all carriers to fulfill a list of "duties" that include interconnection with other carriers.

➤ Lists a set of "obligations" of all local exchange carriers. These include resale, number portability, dialing parity, access to rights of way, reciprocal compensation, unbundled access, and collocation for competitor network equipment.

➤ Requires that manufacturers and telecommunications service providers ensure that their equipment or service is accessible to the disabled, if this is readily achievable, or that equipment and services are compatible with existing devices used by the disabled.

➤ Mandates that the FCC institute and refer to a federal-state joint board a proceeding to recommend changes to any of its regulations pertaining to universal service.

➤ States that regional holding companies (RHCs) may also provide video services for both in-region and out-of-region customers and engage in manufacturing of equipment, but through separate subsidiaries.

➤ Regulates how the Regional Bell Operating Companies (RBOCs) may offer out-of-region interLATA services — services between local access and transport areas (LATAs), or, more simply, long-distance service. An RBOC may offer out-of-region interLATA services, but before it can offer in-region interLATA services it must provide evidence that it has satisfied the conditions of a 13-point checklist, which states that it must:

1. Allow interconnection
2. Allow access to its networks
3. Allow access to poles, conduits, and other rights-of-way
4. Unbundle local-loop transmission from other services
5. Unbundle trunk-side transport from switching
6. Unbundle local switching from transport, local-loop transmission, or their services
7. Provide nondiscriminatory access to 911, directory, and operator call completion services
8. Provide white pages directory for other carriers
9. Provide number portability
10. Provide access to information necessary for signaling, call routing, and completion
11. Provide dialing parity
12. Offer reciprocal compensation
13. Offer telecommunications resale.

Title II. Broadcast Services

➤ Allows immediate increased ownership of radio stations in local markets.

➤ Stipulates that an entity may own enough television stations to reach 35 percent of a national audience, but the FCC will determine the appropriate limit of ownership of television stations in each specific local market.

➤ Directs the FCC to permit network/cable cross-ownership and removes the prohibition on cable operators owning or controlling local broadcast systems.

Title III. Cable Services

➤ Ends rate regulation of most cable television programming by March 31, 1999.

➤ Allows local exchange companies to provide cable service to cable subscribers in their telephone service areas.

➤ Repeals the telephone companies/cable cross-ownership restriction imposed by the 1984 Cable Act.

➤ States that certified open video system (OVS) providers are subject to reduced regulation.

Title IV. Regulatory Reform

➤ Stipulates that "the FCC shall forbear from enforcing any regulation or provision of the Act to a telecommunications carrier or telecommunications service, or class thereof, in any or some of its geographic markets, if the FCC finds that such forbearance is not necessary to ensure that rates are just and reasonable, that enforcement of such regulation is not necessary for the protection of consumers, and that forbearance from enforcement of such regulation is in the public interest."

Title V. Broadcast Obscenity and Violence

➤ Prescribes the establishment of an advisory committee for the rating of video programming that contains indecent materials for purposes of parental control. Within two years, all televisions with screens 13 inches or larger must be equipped with a "V chip" to allow parents to block programs with a predesignated rating.

Title VI. Effect on Other Laws

➤ States that nothing in the act shall be construed to impair, modify, or supersede the application of the antitrust laws.

➤ Stipulates that "any conduct or activity that was, before the date of enactment of the 1996 Act, subject to any restriction or obligation imposed by the AT&T Consent Decree, the GTE Consent Decree or the Mc-Caw Consent Decree shall, on and after such date, be subject to the restrictions and obligations imposed by the Communications Act of 1934, as amended by the 1996 Act."

Title VII. Miscellaneous Provisions

➤ Prohibits unfair billing practices
➤ Mandates that telecommunications carriers protect the confidentiality of proprietary customer information.

to new entrants at cost-based prices, and to provide service at wholesale prices to new competitors so they could gain a foothold in the local service market through resale of services to customers. Significantly, the act forbids the RBOCs from entering the long-distance services market in their respective regions until they have complied with all of its provisions to the satisfaction of the FCC. The RBOCs have been barred from that market since the 1984 antitrust settlement that resulted in their divestiture from AT&T.

What's been the upshot of the Telecommunications Act? According to a 1999 report from the Council of Economic Advisors, there has been considerable activity at the local service level. A flurry of new carriers has entered the wireline local market (see Figure 5.1), providing both switched voice and high-speed data services to customers. Nationally, these competitive local exchange carriers have captured between 2 and 3% of the local services market as measured by lines, and about 5% of the market as measured by revenues. What's more, they have created more than 50,000 jobs and generated more than $30 billion in capital investment, not counting debt and private venture financing.

A further accounting shows that resale of incumbents' services is the primary vehicle by which the CLECs are currently serving residential customers. But as the CLECs continue to build out fiber networks at a rapid clip, it's clear that their ability to serve customers over their own networks will grow tremendously. Although the CLECs are still in the early stages of accumulating market share — only a handful have so far posted a profit — they are responsible for nearly 20% of the growth in the local telecommunications market since 1993, according to the Council of Economic Advisors.

On the wireless side of the business, the remarkable growth that began in the early 1990s has intensified since the passage of the U.S. Telecommunications Act, which allowed providers to bundle roaming, local, and long-distance service on virtually any terms they wanted. It was actually in 1983 that the FCC assigned the first licenses to use the radio spectrum for cellular telephone service. It introduced competition through a "duopoly rule" under which one license in each geographic market was given to the incumbent local telephone provider, and another to an unaffiliated competitor. By June 1985, cellular companies collectively had over 200,000 subscribers, 600 cell sites (each site contains the transmission equipment that serves a local cell), and 1,700 employees. Ten years later, the wireless industry took another major step as the FCC held the

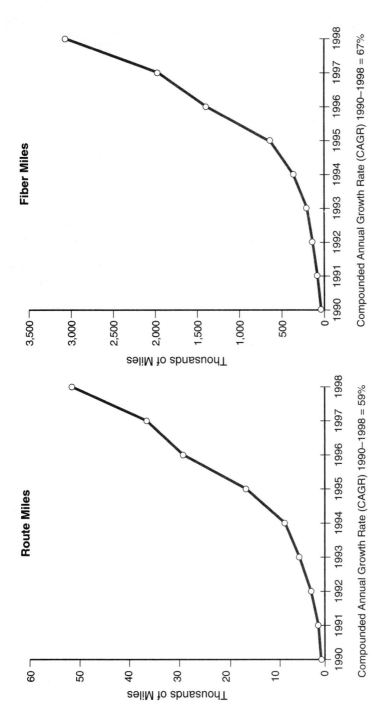

Figure 5.1 CLEC Network Build-Outs

Source: Federal Communications Commission

first auctions for broadband spectrum to be used for digital personal communication services (PCS), creating a new wave of wireless licensees in the U.S. market. As these successful bidders entered the market, and as subsequent licenses were auctioned, the original duopoly market structure turned into full-fledged competition among a host of cellular providers, large and small.

The upshot is that by the middle of 1998, there were nearly 61 million cellular subscribers (see Figure 5.2)—or more than one in four adults—over 57,000 cell sites, and some 135,000 employees (see Figure 5.3) with wireless telephone companies. Increasing competition, improving technology, continuing investments (see Figure 5.4), and declining prices have provoked a new groundswell: people are starting to use their cellular phones as a substitute for wireline service. And as that trend intensifies, it spells monstrous changes ahead for the telecommunications industry.

What will also spell epochal change for the industry, of course, is the entry of the Baby Bells into the long-distance market. In crafting the 1996 Telecommunications Act, regulators developed a checklist of some 13 items the Bells must meet to demonstrate their commitment to a fully competitive local exchange market (see the sidebar, "The Telecommunications Act of 1996"). All these changes are required of the regional carriers to enable the CLECs to interact with their networks. When, and only when, this checklist is complied with would the incumbents be allowed passage into the world of long-distance, the government ruled.

While the standard to which the Baby Bells are being held is presumably based on competition, I believe it has evolved into something else. It now seems to be based more on evaluating the amount of market share the incumbents have lost to other carriers. To my mind, that is an inherently flawed method of determining their suitability to become long-distance players, because some of the biggest losses for the RBOCs are occurring among their business

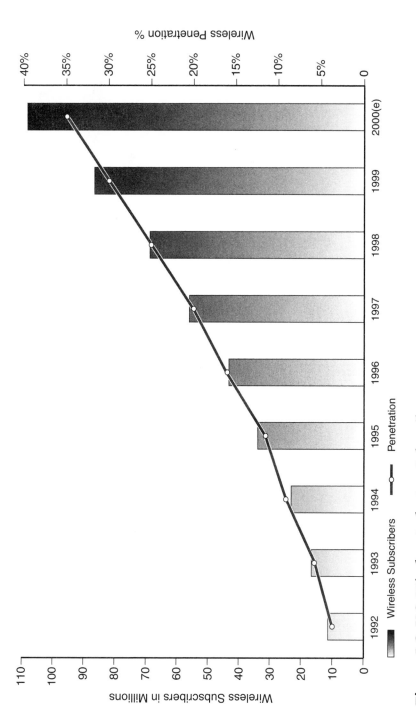

Figure 5.2 U.S. Wireless Industry: Subscribers

Sources: Cellular Telecommunications Industry Association, The Yankee Group

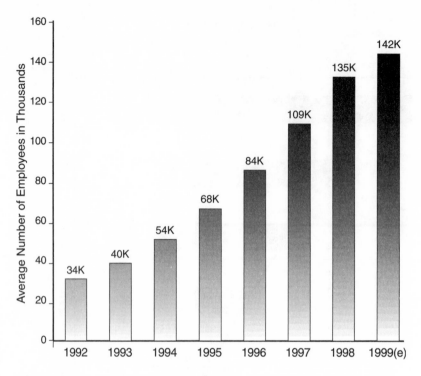

Figure 5.3 U.S. Wireless Industry: Employment Growth

Source: Cellular Telecommunications Industry Association's Wireless Industry Survey Results

customers and high-end residential users, which happen to be their most profitable accounts. Thus, a market share loss of 5% could actually translate into a profit loss of 10% given the breadth of the departing accounts. So, if market share is going to be used as a criterion for judging the performance of the incumbents, regulators must, in all fairness, also weigh the impact of any lost share on the profitability of the carriers. And that could put the RBOCs in a far different competitive light.

Regardless of the mechanism used, the Holy Grail is finally within sight for the incumbents. In late 1999, Bell Atlantic, now Verizon Communications, won FCC approval to offer long-distance service to the 6.6 million households it

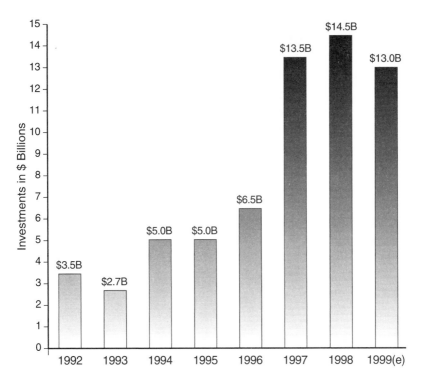

Figure 5.4 U.S. Wireless Industry: Annual Capital Investments

Source: Cellular Telecommunications Industry Association

serves in New York State. This marked not only the first such approval for a Baby Bell, but the first time since the breakup of AT&T in 1984 that consumers would be able to get both local and long-distance phone service from the same carrier. Bell Atlantic's entry into the long-distance market is a very positive and long-overdue development, indeed. For the sooner the Baby Bells are allowed into the long-distance lane, and interexchange carriers (IXCs) like AT&T have unencumbered access to the local lane, the sooner the full competitive intent of the Telecommunications Act of 1996 will be realized.

■ WHEN NATIONAL CONTROL MATTERS

At the same time they are playing a less intrusive role in some areas, regulators should clearly be taking a more aggressive stance in others. One example is universal service, where the demonstrable pitfalls of trying to execute a program with 50 different state jurisdictions in charge makes a very convincing case for strong, national direction. Also in need of a centralized hand is the effort to overhaul outdated industry rules to reflect the realities of a fast-converging marketplace. While the Telecommunications Act took a step in this direction, a tremendous amount of work remains to create a perfectly level playing field.

Here's a more detailed discussion of each of these important areas.

➤ Standardizing the Rules

At a recent conference, I heard a speaker from one of the large telcos cite an interesting fact. Cable television companies can run their coaxial or fiber optic lines right into a multihousing unit without the prior approval of the landlord. Fixed wireline companies can't; they must first secure the landlord's approval. And that got me to thinking: There must be a number of other discrepancies in the rules that govern the cable and telephone industries — discrepancies that directly impact how effectively companies are able to compete.

That is an area where the FCC can play a valuable and essential role. Regulations governing these industries were developed in very different times to reflect very different market conditions. With these industries now converging (there is no better example than AT&T and its recent cable acquisitions), it's high time for regulators to take a fresh and critical look at the ground rules. I'm not necessarily suggesting the FCC overturn what now exists. What I am suggesting is that, at the very least, the agency reevaluate the current standards with an eye toward changing those that (1) provide an unfair competitive advantage for one industry segment over another, or (2) are just plain antiquated in today's communications environment. By fostering greater uniformity and standardization among these major industries, the FCC will go a long way toward ensuring a strong and healthy communications sector for the twenty-first century.

➤ Universal Service

Another area that regulators must carefully rethink in light of changing industry conditions is *universal service*. Under universal service, communications service providers have an obligation to ensure that everyone in their serving areas has access to basic telecommunications services. This translates into subsidized services for low-income and disabled individuals, as well as for customers living in rural (high-cost) service areas. Universal service, as spelled out in the Telecommunications Act of 1996, also includes assistance to schools, libraries, and other public institutions to ensure they have access to the latest telecommunications services.

As presently interpreted, universal service is a major cost center for many local telecom providers. Much concern revolves around who will be responsible — and to what extent — for supporting universal service as new competitors enter the marketplace. In many cases, that support is now shared by the competitors providing service in a given territory. Few people in the industry would probably object to the principle behind universal service: opening up the telecom system to people who might otherwise be unable to afford it. In terms of its actual funding and administration, however, universal service strikes many as antiquated and in sore need of updating. Because it is managed through a complex system of support mechanisms at the state public utility level, it has — predictably — become a jumble of local programs that in at least one case, California, has produced such a surfeit of money that state officials are hard-pressed to know how to spend it. To some industry observers, universal service is little more than a hidden tax that effectively limits the carriers in their efforts to reduce residential telecommunications fees.

Change is in the air. The Telecommunications Act of 1996 called on the FCC and the state public utility commissions to work together to design and implement a new framework for universal service. FCC Chairman Kennard has expressed his support for a revised universal service program that is "competitively neutral"; in other words, one that does not favor or unduly burden one company over another. That is an encouraging sign. But in their deliberations over universal service, regulators must be ever mindful of the complexities involved in funding any new system in light of the rapid changes within the industry. More to the point, they must realize that subsidized communications services are a function of price, and that steadily declining telecom costs and prices will effectively reduce the pool of individuals who require the benefits of universal service. Clearly, any universal service funding mechanism that's developed by the government must take the industry's falling prices into account: Individuals who cannot afford telecom service at today's prices may find it eminently affordable at tomorrow's.

There's another key lesson to be learned from our example of universal service, I believe. And that's the pressing need for a national structure to implement regulations within an industry that is fast becoming borderless. It must be the role of the FCC to get behind the driver's seat of universal service and turn it into a program that is fair and equitable not only for consumers, but for the telecommunications service providers who are required to fund it.

■ THE BREWING STORM OVER OPEN ACCESS

Another area where the need for central direction is becoming increasingly apparent is the tinderbox issue known as *open access,* or "the last mile." In the middle of this issue is AT&T which, through its acquisition of cable giants TCI and MediaOne, controls the pipe reaching into 26 million American homes. Open access poses the question: Should AT&T and other cable companies—which are spending billions of dollars to upgrade their cable systems to provide high-speed Internet access to customers—be obliged to open their networks to competitors, such as America Online and other ISPs? Some customers of AT&T's cable service currently pay a set monthly fee for that fast Internet access bundled with Excite@Home, the online service that AT&T partially owns. While those customers can subscribe to another ISP, such as America Online, to do so they must first pay an additional monthly fee.

America Online and the other Internet service providers are keenly aware of the need for broadband access if they are to successfully compete in the future. That requirement was a major driver in AOL's recent decision to tie the knot with Time Warner, thus gaining access to one of the nation's leading cable systems. What the ISPs want is the ability to buy capacity on the large cable systems at wholesale prices and then resell it to consumers—bundled, of course, with their own Internet content.

AT&T and the cable industry are hardly sympathetic. The company points out that it spent more than $100 billion to acquire its new cable franchise, and is laying out billions more to ensure that its system has the ability to handle high-speed Internet service, as well as telephone traffic. Collectively, the cable industry is spending in excess of $36 billion to refurbish its network for an Internet future, and argues that this magnitude of private investment warrants some level of protection from outside incursions.

The flashpoint for open access was a court ruling in

Portland, Oregon, that forced AT&T to open up its TCI cable network to any competitor willing to pay for its usage. AT&T has challenged the ruling but, ominously for the company, hundreds of pitched battles could lie ahead as communities across the country take up the open access issue.

Interestingly, AOL and Time Warner said following their merger that they intend to provide open access over their combined systems. This, of course, would put pressure on AT&T to go down the same path, though it is too soon to foresee the full impact of this new development.

The following point must be made: While cable is shaping up as the preferred conduit for bringing broadband to U.S. households, it is by no means the only conduit. Telephone companies are starting to roll out a major competitive technology, digital subscriber line (DSL) service, which turns standard copper phone wires into high-capacity pipes with the ability to handle web surfing and phone calls simultaneously. As part of a strategy to make sure it has all bases covered, AOL struck deals with Verizon Communications and SBC Communications Corporation to piggyback its service with their emerging DSL links. In addition to DSL, satellite and wireless are emerging as ways of technologically bridging the last mile. AOL has also agreed to invest $1.5 billion in Hughes Electronics Corporation, which owns DirecTV, a two-way satellite service that could deliver high-speed Internet access to AOL customers.

Where does all this jockeying leave regulators and, more important, the public? The answer for now: sitting squarely on the fence, which I feel is the appropriate short-term place to be. Truth is, no one knows how this broadband access game is going to play out. Will it be cable or will it be DSL? It could well be a combination of both. While handicappers might give cable the edge at present, DSL is gaining ground as the RBOCs begin to more aggressively deploy this network technology—technology that seems able to hold its own in the marketplace.

The overarching issue throughout the unfolding debate is ensuring that consumers have the most effective high-speed vehicle for bringing the digital revolution into their homes. And any efforts by the government at this early stage to regulate access could well serve to choke off further private investment in developing and improving last mile facilities.

The FCC, I believe, is wise in taking a wait-and-see posture. It should be going slower rather than faster when it comes to open access, until more is known about the evolving broadband technologies and their impact on competition and pricing. If it turns out that cable is the dominant technology—to the exclusion of DSL, wireless broadband and other high-speed services—then I believe the government would be well advised to consider regulating the last mile to ensure that no single company has a stranglehold on the market and on pricing. If, however, the last mile is open to a range of competitive access technologies, and consumers have a clear-cut choice, then the need for regulatory control is obviously diminished.

Another factor in the equation, however, should be the staggering cost of infrastructure development. What the United States wants to avoid is the kind of gross overspending that's taken place in Australia, where local newspapers have reported how two cable companies, Optus and Fox, have been laying cable side-by-side, passing nearly every house in the country's largest cities, competing head-to-head on the basis of content. The result is an approximately $30 billion cable network in a relatively small country that could have developed comparable service for a fraction of that bloated cost.

Longer term, it is clear the government in the United States will have to actively come to grips with the open access issue. Without some central direction, the country will be faced with hundreds of Portland-type battles as community after community attempts to resolve open access on its own terms. That would be a terrible diversion from the real business at hand, which is building the best possible high-speed network for the public. If anything is clear at this point, it is that open access is an issue that will demand a strong national focus. Leaving open access decisions to the individual states and their public utility commissions is an invitation to confusion and disarray. The FCC must ultimately step up to the plate and settle the open access issue in a decisive way—one that meets both the short- and the long-term interests of consumers and the communications industry.

■ A SUPPORTIVE ROLE FOR GOVERNMENT

Although deregulation is the global catchword for the communications industry, it is not inconsistent to suggest that government ought to play a more active role in certain critical areas. One of those is research and development. Many industries in the United States have never excelled at basic research and development. Companies have done much better at taking ideas fresh off the drawing board and implementing them in a practical, commercial way. Government, on the other hand, has an enviable record of achievement in the research arena. There are NASA's glowing successes, for example, in the field of manned spaceflight and exploration, the advances of the National Institutes of Health in cancer research and other therapeutic fields, and, lest we forget, the government's key role in creating the Internet.

There is every reason to believe that the government, through its massive resources and basic research prowess, could contribute mightily to the future growth and strength of the telecom industry. By encouraging and funding R&D through collaborative programs with industry/academia—programs like Internet 2, which is developing the next-generation Internet—it can set the stage for breakthrough products, services, and networks designed to keep the United States in the forefront of telecommunications for many years to come. Both industry and government should actively look for ways to develop this kind of partnership, in order to integrate their research skills and resources in a way that builds the strongest possible telecommunications franchise.

The government can support the industry in another powerful way: by being sensitive to the needs of U.S. communications companies that are pursuing major alliances and acquisitions as a way of gaining the bulk necessary to take on competitors anywhere in the world. In ruling on these proposed deals, the FCC would do well to consider the legitimate need that exists among these players for size and scale. Ultimately, what's at stake here is more than just enabling a bunch of large companies to grow even larger. It's the ability of an industry that is one of this country's brightest lights to effectively shine — and compete — on the $800 billion global telecom stage.

Chapter **6**

Driving Toward Customer-Managed

Customer service is not a term that glides loosely off the telecommunications tongue. That is not surprising, given that service providers have historically been tethered not to customers, but to regulators, who set the rules and guidelines by which the monopolistic telecom industry and its practitioners played. Indeed, elaborate organizational structures were put in place to respond to the needs and requirements of regulatory bodies. Billing is a good example. It has become over the years the single biggest operating expenditure in the budgets of the providers as they deployed the necessary machinery to bill on an item-by-item basis and attempt to make sense of the nearly impenetrable maze of pricing schedules that developed.

Fundamental changes are now under way. As a result of growing competition across telephone markets in this country, regulators are yielding to customers and complacency is giving way to enterprise as the telcos seek to hone their customer service capability. It's a sign of the changing times that nearly all providers today purport to be "customer-driven," "customer-focused," or "customer-centric." The reality, however, is quite different.

Predictably, the major long-distance companies are furthest along the customer service curve inasmuch as they have been in a competitive mode the longest. Companies like AT&T, MCI WorldCom, and Sprint recognize the need for customer obsession, and are settling into a stage known as customer care. The vast majority of the communications industry, however, is still basically cutting its teeth when it comes to addressing customer needs. Many companies, particularly the newer competitive local exchange carriers (CLECs) and Internet service providers (ISPs), remain at the earliest stage of competition on the basis of price, while others have moved on to competing via services and quality of service.

No company, though—not even the industry titans— comes close to approaching the level of customer service that I feel will be essential to effectively competing and winning in the twenty-first century. That stage is a newly defined end point on the customer service continuum, a radical new way of thinking about and responding to the customer, which I refer to as *customer-managed.*

For a carrier like AT&T, customer-managed won't mean just being a dependable company with the best interests of its customers in mind. It will mean being *millions* of dependable companies that are able to individually define themselves around the specific needs of every last residential and business customer of AT&T. It will mean recognizing the needs of customers even before they do, and having solutions at the ready. Finally, it will mean knowing the customer's hot buttons, and proactively taking steps to defuse or correct problems before they escalate into major confrontations.

Think of it this way. Customer-managed isn't just knowing your client and holding their hand. It's letting the customer actually define the relationship on the basis of services, billing, pricing, and a host of other factors, then reengineering your business around that definition to deliver what the customer wants. It isn't just being flexible and responsive to customer needs: It's making a company look like a personal service provider to each customer. It's having the resources and resolve to address a market segment of one.

■ THE ROAD TO CUSTOMER-MANAGED

How does a company get to customer-managed? There is no clearly marked road map, though it may be helpful to examine the four competitive stages for gaining market share to understand the vast length of roadway that must be traversed. This model was developed by KPMG based on analyses of various telecommunications markets as they deregulated—one of the most prominent being the long-distance telephone market in the United States.

1. *Pricing*—In the early stages of the customer relationship, price is paramount. In fact, it's often the reason a customer changes telecommunications service providers in the first place. A new entrant to the local market, for example, might cultivate a growing customer base by undercutting the incumbent provider 30% on price. What normally occurs over time, however, is that the incumbent lowers its price, too, and the issue quickly fades as a competitive strategy. Companies start scrambling for other tactical positions.

2. *New services*—This stage typically follows. The new carrier's strategy might be, "Okay, AT&T has met me on price, so now I'm going to do them one better. I'm going to offer my customers an array of new services that are going to make their lives easier, like breaking out their bills by business and personal calls, or giving them caller ID as part of their basic service package." But as you'd expect, the incumbents soon catch up and, before long, everyone is offering more or less the same repertoire of services at roughly the same prices.

3. *Quality of service*—Bereft of price and new services as defining issues, service quality now comes into the competitive crosshairs. Through programs like Sprint's Pin Drop and AT&T's TrueVoice, carriers

make their "exclusive" claims to superior service levels, as evidenced by purportedly clearer telephone lines, fewer dropped calls, faster customer service, and so forth. Those claims may in fact be true, but with time, even quality fades as a distinguishing factor as technology along with improved staffing and training tend to level the competitive playing field.

4. *Customer care*—This stage represents a major step down the road to impassioned customer service. It refocuses the company on responding to customer needs in a more timely fashion, though within the context of the current business model. Call centers might be infused with new customer-friendly technology, for example, or technicians trained in how to recognize and respond to gaps in customer service levels. The goal behind customer care is to provide an excellent experience for the customer every time he or she interacts with your company. (See Figure 6.1.)

■ BREAKING THE MOLD

While customer care is generally seen as the desired endpoint of customer service, in the future it will be little more than an interim step on the road to customer-managed. The distance between those two mileposts, however, is far from incremental: They're light years apart. For carriers to bridge the chasm between reactive customer care and proactive customer-managed will require massive changes in the way they operate, structure, and think about their businesses. It will oblige them to throw away all the old rules and essentially start with a blank sheet of paper. In this fertile environment, out-of-the-box thinking will be not only desirable but essential.

For example, customer-managed will lead businesses away from the traditional approach keyed to individual products, features, and benefits to one that's built on how

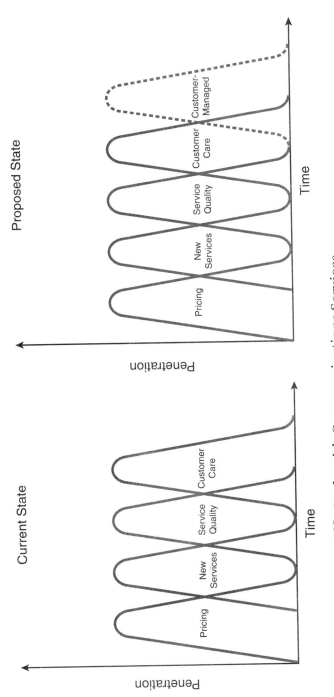

Figure 6.1 Customer Life Cycle with Communications Services

Source: KPMG Research

those products fit into an integrated *solution* aimed at solving a customer problem or meeting a complex need. This will require another fundamental change of telecom providers: that they start dealing with their customers on an enterprisewide basis. No longer will customers be the exclusive preserve of data networking, wireless, or wireline divisions. They will belong to the entire business, meaning that every division and every function—from maintenance and repair to billing and accounting to field sales and call centers—will have a hand in defining, building, and perfecting the customer relationship.

While each communications company will invariably leave its imprint on customer-managed, several universal pillars are critical to and will strongly support their endeavors. They are systems, pricing, and strategic alliances. Following is a more detailed look at each.

➤ Systems Support

Let's start with this premise: Powerful operating and business systems are the sine qua non of customer-managed. Indeed, customer-managed is possible only because of the advanced technologies now available to help businesses effectively manage such applications as customer service, billing, accounting, and support. In the past, many of these systems were considered back office, their sole mission processing information and summarizing data for internal use. Under customer-managed, these support systems will play a far different role. They will assume a powerful position right on the front line, giving the communications provider and even customers themselves an effective set of tools to manage costs and control service levels.

A good example is the telephone company call centers to which customers report problems or call in to rearrange their service or ask a billing question. Many telcos have multiple call centers—one for wireline, another for wireless, another for card services, and so on. If I initiate a trouble call, the appropriate call center will ask for my telephone number and verify that I am one of its customers. However, they usually have no way of knowing if I have multiple service relationships with the parent company since many of their systems are set up to recognize only a ten-digit phone number, not a universal customer identification code.

Customer-managed will put that systems capability to work in a much more aggressive—and productive—way. Through a consistent ID number that sticks to me across all lines of business, the call center representative will know immediately which services I have and which I don't. In short, I will be an enterprisewide customer. And that, in turn, will open up a plethora of proactive service and sales opportunities for the communications provider. Contacting a call center seeking problem resolution might also yield an offer such as: "We notice, Mr. Bonocore, that you have wireless service in addition to wireline, and we'd like to suggest to you a package at ten cents a minute for both services that could save you a considerable amount of money each month." A call center representative's access to the right systems information could also provide an opening for a statement such as: "Are you aware, Mr. Bonocore, that 15 people called your number last month but hung up without leaving a message? You might want to consider call waiting or voice mail service as a way of preventing those lost phone calls from routinely occurring." The benefits are unmistakable: not only does the customer get more attentive, personalized service, but the provider is able to capture a wealth of new sales opportunities via its existing call center staff.

Technology will help structure the customer-managed relationship in a number of other important ways. By responding at the outset to what might be described as a questionnaire or instruction set, customers will enable the communications provider to explicitly define their needs, then marshal its considerable resources around them. For example, those instructions will enable customers to specify on what day of the month they want to receive their bill, how they want to receive it (online, fax, or mail), and what level of service detail or quality of service they require. Business customers, for their part, will be able to assign telephone costs to specific lines of business, profit centers, or departments, or prescribe the kinds of Internet access or telephone calling privileges that employees or groups of employees should have as a way of holding down costs and preventing abuse. They will also be able to obtain any of dozens of standard reports detailing their call activity and other information that might help them run their businesses more efficiently.

One of the earliest and most impressive demonstrations of technology's influence on the customer relationship was MCI's Friends & Family. With its splashy introduction in the mid-1980s, this cleverly conceived program forever changed the shape of the long-distance market. The concept was relatively simple: when a customer signed up friends and family as part of the program, all group members received a 20% discount on any long-distance calls made intragroup. Representing the first dramatic reduction in telephone long-distance rates, Friends & Family was essentially a billing service. It took what had been for MCI a back-office systems function and gave it front-line utility — and respectability. Friends & Family was a major marketing coup for MCI that helped it take significant market share away from the competition. AT&T, for its part, was caught flat-footed and unprepared via its billing system to mount an effective response. Perhaps even more revealing, Friends & Family shows what can happen when companies are willing to throw tradition to the wind and start with a clean slate. In other words, when they are willing to change the paradigm.

Sound a little like customer-managed?

MCI WorldCom's Friends & Family

Friends & Family, launched in March 1991, was a watershed for the telecommunications industry. This bold program marked a departure from the incessant rounds of price-cutting in force since the inception of competition, and placed new emphasis on service differentiation. It was also the first time a carrier used its customer information database as a full-fledged tool to generate business, not merely collect revenues.

Friends & Family gave MCI WorldCom customers a 20% discount on their most frequent long-distance calls, providing both they and the called party were subscribers to the program. From each participant, MCI WorldCom got a list of family and friends they would like to see on their discount calling plan. The company then used this information to encourage these prospects to enroll and, just as important, start their own Friends & Family list. This created what is called an infinitely progressive database—almost like a chain letter—with a virtually endless supply of new prospects and customers.

Thanks to Friends & Family, MCI WorldCom is believed to have gained a 2% long-distance market share—an increase of more than $1.2 billion in incremental revenue in 1991 alone. According to MCI WorldCom, the company signed up 10 million new customers in 1991 and 1992, the first two years of Friends & Family. That remarkable success prompted the program's extension to MCI Mail, the company's electronic mail product, as well as to its paging service. And in 1994, MCI introduced Friends & Family mail (separate from MCI Mail), which entitles MCI WorldCom's long-distance Friends & Family customers to 10 free e-mail messages a month.

➤ The Pricing Advantage

A sea change is also under way in the pricing of communications services. Historically, carriers determined what it cost them to provide a service, then went to the local regulators to negotiate a margin or fee over and above the cost of the service. This calculation determined the rate that the carrier could charge customers for the service.

In an increasingly deregulated environment, competition is setting the parameters for how communications services are priced. Under customer-managed, the model will experience further radical change. That's because customers themselves—supplied with the appropriate tools and options—will control the pricing of their services. For example, by routing the bulk of their data traffic overnight rather than during the day, or by creating a package that adds wireless to existing wireline service, customers will have the flexibility to determine their service levels along with the prices they pay.

Customers are already reaping the rewards of sweeping changes to telecom pricing. As carriers begin to offer a panoply of services under "one roof," they are offering pricing plans that encourage cross-selling and increased usage of those services. The current trend is toward pricing all services at a simplified flat rate per minute. AT&T's One Rate Plan, for instance, combines long distance, calling card, and wireless into one monthly charge, plus a standard fee per minute of usage.

Despite all the hoopla, though, I don't believe the industry is headed toward simplification. Rather than supporting fewer pricing plans, customer-managed will engender *countless* plans as each service provider crafts its unique offerings to cater to the specific needs of each customer. For that reason, I would find it extremely desirable as a communications company today to be the first in my field to offer customers the tools to access and evaluate my company's pricing plans versus those of the competition. Aside from winning points for openness and imagination, I would gain incredible exposure for my service offerings. Moreover, I would find myself receiving some highly useful information that could enable me to modify and update my pricing plans on an ongoing basis.

➤ The Role of Alliances and Acquisitions

Although customer-managed will be a boon to communications users, it will pose a daunting challenge to service providers. Few if any companies will be able to marshal the overwhelming array of services, options, and capabilities needed to drive customer-managed. More than ever, providers will have to look outside their walls for a strong supporting cast. And that, I believe, will lead inexorably to strategic alliances and acquisitions.

The tidal wave of consolidations that's sweeping the industry (see Chapter 2, "The Demolition-Rebuilding Process") confirms one of its basic new truths: Size and scale matter. It's clear that only the largest and best-equipped players will be able to offer a full range of services over a fully integrated, seamless network, or be able to achieve the economies of scale needed to provide competitive pricing and superior customer service.

Over the near term, strategic alliances and acquisitions are enabling their principals to fill out their national footprints and achieve critical mass. Over the longer term, however, they may be benefiting in a way that most are probably not even aware of at present: By consolidating, they're gaining the extraordinary resources they'll need to make customer-managed a reality.

■ THE BANKING BENCHMARK

Communications is only one of many industries awakening to the need for a strong customer orientation. Banking felt the sobering winds of change a number of years ago, and has begun to respond convincingly. The parallels between the two industries are considerable. Both come from tightly regulated backgrounds, both are now searching for bold new ways to refocus on the customer, and both are increasingly reliant on technology to realize their goals. In a number of areas like the development of enterprisewide customers, however, banking has moved noticeably ahead of telecom. For that reason, it's helpful to peruse the fast-changing banking landscape for tactical clues and lessons learned.

Like telecom, banking realized that the old industry model had become as dated as green eyeshades and toaster giveaways. Conventional banking—where institutions took deposits and made loans—had become a commodity business with razor-thin margins. In the new scheme of things, banks were no longer just banks, but financial services institutions founded on the notion of fast, easy, convenient solutions for customers.

Wells Fargo, for example, began closing traditional branches in the mid-1990s and opening scores of more economical and customer-convenient minibanks in high-traffic areas like supermarkets, drugstores, and department stores. By 1998, the growing reliance on minibranches had enabled Wells Fargo to double its retail outlets in California alone to more than 1,200.

As part of its growing affinity for customers, Wells Fargo undertook an earnest effort to determine what makes them tick. More specifically, it developed an elaborate computer model to track customers' banking behavior, and used that information in a marketing-savvy way. Customers who used ATMs for everything but deposits were contacted to get them more comfortable with depositing by machine. Customers who constantly used tellers were informed of the alternatives. The model was particularly effective at pinpointing customers considered to be at risk of fleeing to the competition, based on their banking habits, thus enabling the bank to proactively take steps to reduce that risk.

First Union, the nation's sixth-largest bank, with a territory stretching from Connecticut to Key West, Florida, also affords an interesting case study. Beginning in 1985, First Union embarked on a growth program that provided geographic penetration into a host of states covering a third of the total population of the United States. In the mid-1990s, it took an even bolder step by redefining the notion of a "bank" and the unique role First Union could play. What emerged was an imaginative concept—Future Bank—built on a simple yet evocative platform: Let customers do business with the bank when, where, and how they prefer.

Under this new model, customers were no longer pigeonholed as checking, savings, or loan. Rather, they were treated as enterprisewide customers with a need for broad financial solutions at any and all stages of their lives. For consumers, these ranged from traditional checking and loan products to wealth management services, including mutual funds, annuities, brokerage, and personal trust. At the same time, First Union customers were being offered an unprecedented range of choices guaranteeing greater convenience and personal control. For example, they could now manage their accounts through any of the bank's 2,400 full-service financial centers or its 3,500 automated teller machines; the Internet at www.firstunion.com; a state-of-the-art telephone banking system offering 24-hour-a-day, seven-day-a-week access; or a brokerage network consisting of 4,300 licensed representatives.

By essentially rebuilding from scratch, First Union was determined to not just grow sales. It was determined to grow lifelong customers.

■ PLANTING THE SEEDS OF CUSTOMER-MANAGED

It is clear that parts of the communications industry, too, are starting to think along customer-managed lines. A number of service providers have developed programs that give customers greatly increased control over day-to-day management of their accounts, particularly in areas like billing and information access.

For example, Teligent, the local and long-distance Internet access company with a fast-growing national base, has created *e-magine*. This value-added service allows customers to sort their billing data any way they want or need it: by location, phone number, or account code. Customers can download this data and perform trend analyses, spot potential fraud and abuse, and compile summaries or zero in on the fine detail.

AT&T, too, allows customers to perform an increasing number of functions online, such as reviewing their bills on a call-by-call basis, even applying for an automatic discount on any calls that were incorrectly billed or dropped. For business customers, AT&T Billing Edge provides monthly invoice and call detail information in a consistent, easy-to-use database format. It also allows customers to access, depending on their AT&T service, up to 67 standard reports and initiate inquiries designed to provide vital information on customer calling patterns and overall network use.

■ TARGETING THE SUMMIT

For companies that eventually scale the customer-managed summit, the rewards will be enormous. With prices, quality, and services becoming more and more homogenized, customer-managed will be one of the few real market differentiators that communications service providers will have within their grasp. It will position them in a very select class.

Not insignificantly, customer-managed will also enable them to more tightly control costs over the longer term. The cost of acquiring a new customer is dramatically higher than the expense of retaining one. That applies to virtually any industry, as published research shows. Because customer-managed will result in a much more stable customer base, it will relieve service providers of much of the cost pressure associated with new customer acquisition. The technological improvements that are put in place as part of customer-managed will also provide powerful leverage when it comes to curbing costs.

Reaching the customer-managed summit, however, will be anything but easy. With customers (and eventually competition) driving the process, the route will be more complex and demanding than anything the service providers have probably experienced. It will require that carriers rethink and redesign virtually every aspect of their business. That's why I believe that companies with an eye to becoming customer-managed will have to focus on specific market segments, rather than attempt to be all things to all customers. Examples of these segments might include residential, small/intermediate business, large business, complex needs, wireless, wireline, satellite, global service, national service, large cities, military, students, and more. AT&T is in the process of restructuring its operations along such segment lines.

MCI WorldCom has already discovered the value of a market-focused strategy. It decided to zero in on the high-volume data needs of business customers within a number of "super" cities across the country. That decision has ably steered the company's network-building program, a process that began with WorldCom's purchase of MFS Communications in 1996. The acquisition of MFS gave WorldCom a direct, local fiber optic link to numerous business customers, as well as ownership of UUNet, a leading Internet service provider. Since MCI and WorldCom merged in fall 1997, they have intensified their pursuit of business customers by offering value-added services like intranets and Internet access through UUNet. This strategy is having a marked impact: Since the merger, MCI WorldCom's revenues from telephone service have fallen from 68 to 61 percent of total sales, while Internet and corporate data services have grown from 22 percent to 30 percent of overall sales.

■ BYPASSING THE COMPETITIVE BOTTLENECKS

The challenge of redefining their markets presents communications service providers with another valuable opportunity: establishing who their most profitable and promising customers are and, by the same token, who their least profitable and therefore most expendable customers are. That may sound a bit Machiavellian, but there is a sound rationale behind it. Under the cover of today's still heavily regulated industry, new entrants are going to take their fair share of the market away from the incumbents. According to some estimates, revenue losses by the established players could reach 20 to 30 percent, or even higher, over time.

Given that marketplace reality, incumbents must ask themselves: Do we fight this or attempt to turn it to our advantage? I believe most companies should opt for the latter, and that means applying their finite resources to retaining the most profitable customers, and not attempting to spread—and ultimately dilute—them among the entire client population.

Resigned to the inevitable loss in his customer base, one telecom executive assured me that his anticipated revenue shortfall would be fully covered by the sale of new products and services. That's fine, I replied, but an even stronger approach would be to target that core group of accounts the carrier most wants to retain, and expand its product and service offerings around that population.

Ultimately, companies that can make that type of transition will find themselves on a much more direct route to customer-managed. And that could yield another significant payback: Companies may be able to short-circuit the historic linear process for gaining competitive market share (discussed earlier in this chapter) and proceed directly to customer-managed from wherever they currently reside. The real winners in the future will be those businesses that don't get stuck in traffic at the usual bottlenecks, but are able to break away and make customer-managed their next — and final — destination.

Chapter

The Internet Laboratory

Most industries have their experimental space where promising new products and ideas can be exhaustively studied, tested, and refined before they're unleashed on the public. In the pharmaceutical industry, the research and development laboratory harbors new compounds for years while their safety and efficacy are challenged in clinical trials. New automotive models, too, spend years in design and development before they're performance tested on high-speed tracks and under punishing road conditions.

In the case of communications, the experimental laboratory is the Internet. It is providing the industry and its players with the models, tools, and technologies for building the optimal network of the future. Mistakes are being made and gambles being taken along the way, but one thing is clear: The network that finally emerges will be all the more robust thanks to the groundbreaking work of the Internet.

To better understand the relationship between the Internet and the evolving communications network, it's necessary to take a look at the Internet's evolution.

■ CARVING OUT A NEW ARCHITECTURE

Online shopping and chat rooms were the furthest thing from anyone's mind when the Internet was born in the late 1960s. In fact, the seeds were planted by the U.S. Department of Defense, which asked a bunch of computer scientists to discover a way for many computers to communicate without the need for a central machine to serve as the traffic cop. A hub-based system, so the thinking went during this Cold War era, would be too vulnerable to nuclear attack. So the Pentagon decided to fund the ARPANET, an experimental network that initially linked four research labs. In so doing, the government put its money behind a new communications technology known as packet switching.

Father of the Internet

The Internet was born in 1969 with the decidedly uncommercial name of ARPANET. Developed by the Advanced Research Projects Agency (ARPA) of the Department of Defense in conjunction with a group of military contractors and universities, ARPANET was an experimental packet-switched network enabling users to share information and resources across long distances. Of no small significance was the fact it was designed to survive a nuclear attack at a time in history when such a cataclysm was not far from everyone's radar screen.

Initially, ARPANET linked four computers—known as Interface Message Processors (IMPs)—located at the University of California at Los Angeles, Stanford Research Institute at Stanford University, the University of California at Santa Barbara, and the University of Utah. ARPANET continued to expand, and by 1973 consisted of 37 host computers. That same year, the first international connections were made to England and Norway.

From 1973 to 1978, a team of researchers headed by Vinton Cerf at Stanford Research Institute and Robert Kahn of ARPA worked on a set of networking rules, or protocols, that

The network genie was soon out of the bottle. The ARPANET quickly spread to dozens of universities and corporations where scientists and engineers, like artists in the midst of a commissioned work, continued to refine and sculpt the medium to fit their needs. They built programs to help people exchange e-mail, tap into remote databases, and brainstorm via electronic bulletin boards. One of the most important innovations, however, was the communications protocol that gave the medium its name.

The Internet protocol (IP) allowed vast numbers of computer networks to link up and communicate as one through a standardized set of rules that specified format, timing, and sequencing. The full set of protocols, known as

---

would allow for the interconnection of different computer networks. This groundbreaking work resulted in the development of TCP/IP (transmission control protocol/Internet protocol). TCP/IP governs how data is transmitted across networks and enables different types of computer operating systems to share information across a network. In 1983, it became the standard protocol set for computers connecting to the ARPANET. This meant that any smaller network wishing to connect to ARPANET had to abide by TCP/IP, as well. In industry parlance, ARPANET had become a powerful "backbone" network offering interconnectability to smaller networks. Once connected to the backbone, these smaller networks were also connected to each other.

By the mid-1970s, ARPANET became fully operational as the official computer network of the U.S. Department of Defense. In the early 1980s, the network was split into two distinct components: MILNET, to serve the needs of the military, and ARPANET, to support ongoing research.

In 1986, the U.S. National Science Foundation (NSF) created a faster backbone network called NSFNET, linking researchers across the country via five supercomputing centers. Because of the huge success of NSFNET, the government decided to phase out ARPANET. That process was completed in 1990—but not before its offspring, the Internet, had begun its incredible rise to stardom.

TCP/IP (transmission control protocol/Internet protocol), began sweeping through the academic and research communities, then into commercial computing circles through such products as Sun Microsystems workstations. Because TCP/IP is not married to any single computing or communications platform, it offered Internet traffic the potential to move through a multitude of facilities: telephone lines, cable TV, wireless, satellite links. By the late 1980s, millions of computers and thousands of networks were using TCP/IP. That paved the way for the Internet of today, a continuum of millions of computers and hundreds of thousands of networks linked globally.

At the same time, the Internet was undergoing a radical transformation in the way it was used. In its infancy, the Net was considered a kind of techno-craze that joined friends or even strangers for expansive online discussions on myriad subjects. It also let users comb through online libraries, play new games, and swap software. By the early 1990s, however, the Internet had slipped out of the hands of the techies. It became much easier to use and took on a contemporary new look thanks to snazzy graphics and sound. The Internet was now open for business—literally—and was about to become a juggernaut that would forever change the face of commerce.

At first, companies used the electronic medium as a repository for information about their products, services, pricing, and whatever else they wanted to impart to prospective customers. It wasn't long before the interactive capability of the Internet was paving the way for an explosion of online transactions—everything from ordering products to finding a home to auctioning a car to conducting personal banking business. Thus, the term *e-commerce* was born amid predictions by Forrester Research that it could reach $327 billion, or 2.3% of the gross domestic product (GDP), among U.S. businesses alone by 2002. From there, it could jump to as much as 6% of the GDP by 2005, giving the twenty-first century economy a tremendous springboard for growth (see Figure 7.1).

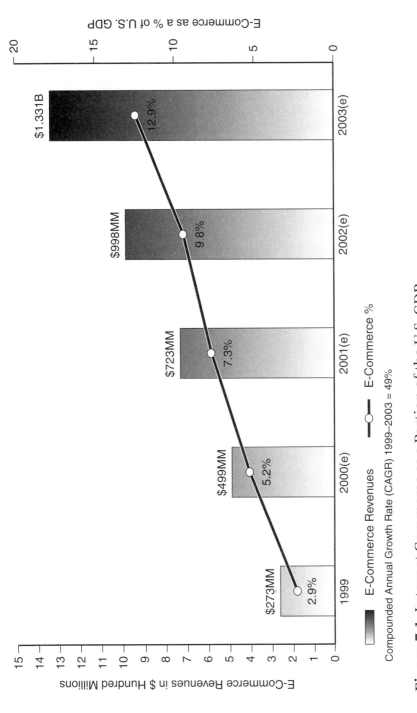

Figure 7.1 Internet Commerce as a Portion of the U.S. GDP

Sources: Forrester Research, Wall Street Journal

The exhilarating next stage of Internet development will make that growth a foregone conclusion. It will parlay a digital blend of data, audio, and video transmission into a new generation of intelligent applications that promises to truly revolutionize the communications network, and provide its players with a powerful source of differentiation. The next chapter, "Building the Network of the Future," explores these points in more detail.

■ THE INTERNET'S WIDENING INFLUENCE

The intense R&D effort unfolding in the Internet lab has already had a powerful impact on the evolving communications network. The effects are most evident in three major areas: transmission, services, and the business model.

➤ Transmission

If there were ever doubts about the future role and importance of data transmission, the Internet has put them to rest. Historically, data transport was defined as large companies sending blocks of digitized information to and between processing sites over private transmission lines. Under the new Internet-crafted definition, data transmission is small packets of information being relayed over high-speed fiber networks that embrace open standards and universal access to link an infinite number of business and residential users. The new megahighway that's making this possible is Internet protocol–based, ensuring fast and economical transport. It's also prepared to integrate voice and video along with data via its wideband capacity to form a truly convergent network for the twenty-first century.

➤ Services

For businesses worldwide, the Internet has opened the door to a new era of flexible and cost-effective services relying on an interactive, dynamic network to reach vast communities of users. These services are redefining how the world of commerce markets, sells, and distributes its products. The Net is allowing companies like Dell and Gateway, for example, to advertise and sell computers via the Net; Charles Schwab & Co. and E*Trade to offer economical online trading from the home; and FedEx to instantaneously schedule and track package pickups and deliveries for its customers. Even IBM has shut down its sale of PCs at retail stores, and migrated instead to the web. (See Figure 7.2 for further examples of how much business is moving online in various industries.)

Cisco Systems, too, neatly illustrates how the Internet is paving the way for a dynamic new world of service solutions. Nearly 78% of that company's orders emanate from the Net — averaging $25 million a day — and of these, nearly half are passed on to manufacturing partners and suppliers without being touched by Cisco personnel. What's more, 71% of all customer support inquiries are handled online, resulting in operating cost savings of approximately $250 million annually.

The network truly is the centerpiece of Cisco's business, seamlessly linking the company to all its constituents: customers, prospects, business partners, suppliers, and employees. Through the network, Cisco makes its worldwide web of partners — including suppliers, contract manufacturers, and assemblers — look like one big, homogeneous company to the outside world. The Net also allows Cisco, the global leader in supplying networking equipment for the Internet, to provide technical assistance to customers worldwide. Access is improved in another important way: by allowing customers to electronically download software. Through this procedure, customers and partners acquire more than 70,000 pieces of software each month, dramatically lowering Cisco's distribution costs while continuing to ensure users access to critical guidance and information 24 hours a day, seven days a week.

➤ Business Model

Some of the most intense research and development on the Internet has been aimed at determining the type of interac-

	Category	1998	1999	2000	2001	2002	2003
Consumer	Media (software, books, music, video)	1.6	3.0	4.7	6.7	8.5	10.0
	Event tickets	0.1	0.2	0.5	1.0	1.7	2.6
	Apparel	0.5	1.3	2.8	5.0	8.3	13.5
	Gifts and flowers	0.3	0.6	0.8	1.1	1.4	1.8
	Recreation (toys, sporting goods, garden)	0.2	0.4	0.8	1.6	2.7	4.4
	Leisure travel	3.1	7.8	14.0	20.7	26.0	29.4
	Electronics and computers	1.2	2.8	5.1	8.4	13.6	21.1
	Housewares	0.1	0.4	1.0	1.9	3.3	5.7
	Food and beverage	0.2	0.5	1.1	2.5	5.0	10.8
	Health and beauty	0.2	0.5	1.2	2.1	3.8	6.3
Business	Aerospace and defense	2.5	6.6	14.8	25.6	34.0	38.2
	Electronics and computers	19.7	50.4	121.4	229.1	319.1	395.3
	Construction	0.4	1.6	3.4	7.0	14.2	28.6
	Consumer goods	1.4	2.8	6.1	12.7	26.0	51.9
	Food and agriculture	0.3	3.0	6.3	13.1	26.7	53.6
	Heavy industries	0.1	1.3	2.5	4.7	8.7	15.8
	Industrial equipment	0.1	1.3	2.4	4.5	8.5	15.8
	Motor vehicles	3.7	9.3	22.7	53.2	114.3	212.9
	Paper and office products	1.3	2.9	6.4	14.3	31.1	65.2
	Petrochemicals	4.7	10.3	22.6	48.0	96.8	178.3
	Pharmaceutical and medical supplies	0.6	1.4	3.5	8.5	20.0	44.1
	Shipping and warehousing	1.2	2.9	6.8	15.4	32.7	61.6
	Utilities	7.1	15.4	32.2	62.9	110.6	169.5

Figure 7.2 Online Business Market Size in $Billions

Source: Consumer: James L. McQuivet, Kaate Delhagen, Kip Levin, and Maria LaTour Kadison, "Retail's Growth Spiral," *The Forrester Report*, November 1998; Business: Steven Bell, Stan Dolberg, Shah Cheema, and Jeremy Sharrard, "Resizing On-Line Business Trade," *The Forrester Report*, November 1998.

tive model that best allows businesses to meet the demands of consumers. These models are more than just network transmission and service vehicles. They are powerful portals—on ramps to the Internet—that employ intelligence resident on the network to enable users to initiate complex transactions in a seamless and secure environment.

Though a number of business models have evolved, vigorous work remains to ascertain which of these is optimally equipped to guide consumers and network developers in the decade ahead—or whether an entirely new one will outstrip the present contenders. The current pacesetters include:

➤ **Amazon.com** is the Net's largest and broadest online consumer retailer, with more than 16 million items (and rapidly growing) for sale. Amazon.com combines fixed prices with a desire to be the most customer-focused electronic merchant. To that end, it invented one-click ordering, which eliminates for consumers time-consuming data entry whenever an order is placed. Buyers simply store credit card and address information after the first purchase. Amazon also aggressively tracks and builds data on each user. In this way, it is able to assess what buyers have purchased and suggest other products they might like. As a result, repeat purchases account for two-thirds of all sales. Significantly, the more data Amazon compiles on each user, the harder it is for competitors to emulate its model.

In its zeal to be customer-driven, Amazon has also built distribution centers around the world to accelerate deliveries to customers. That distribution capability makes it relatively easy for the company to add almost any type of new product.

➤ **eBay** has taken a much different approach than rival Amazon.com. It is the largest person-to-person auction web site, linking people up to buy and sell antiques and collectibles as well as many other goods normally purchased at flea markets and antiques stores. In opting for the auction format, eBay has settled into the role of middleman or broker. It never takes possession of the goods, and thus incurs none of Amazon's sizable distribution costs (a fact reflected in its outsized gross profit margins). eBay simply takes a cut off the top, and operates with a skeletal crew compared to Amazon. eBay can also take comfort in the knowledge that its constituents spend an average of 130 minutes a month at its site, roughly 10 times what Amazon can claim of its cybershoppers.

Letting online consumers and business buyers haggle over all manner of goods and services — from cars and mortgages to clothing and paintings — is perhaps the hottest idea today in the already superheated world of e-commerce. Consumer and business auctions are expected to account for nearly 20% of all e-commerce, or $65 billion, by 2002, up from $10.1 billion at the end of 1998, according to *The Forrester Report* (see Figure 7.3). Increasingly, auctions are involving not just eBay-like consumer-to-consumer purchases, but business-to-consumer transactions, as well. And by 2003, an anticipated $2.1 billion worth of airline tickets and hotel rooms, $1.7 billion of car sales, and $1.2 billion of apparel sales will be generated through online auctions. According to Forrester Research, industrial auctions such as FreeMarkets Online, which sells coal and printed circuit boards to businesses, are growing even faster, from $8.7 billion in 1998 to an anticipated $53 billion by 2002. No wonder Amazon.com decided to go with the flow and begin holding its own daily auctions.

➤ **PriceLine.com** is the standard-bearer of a third distinct e-commerce model. Instead of the fixed pricing of Amazon.com or the dynamic pricing of eBay, it has opted for "real-time" pricing. Consumers name the

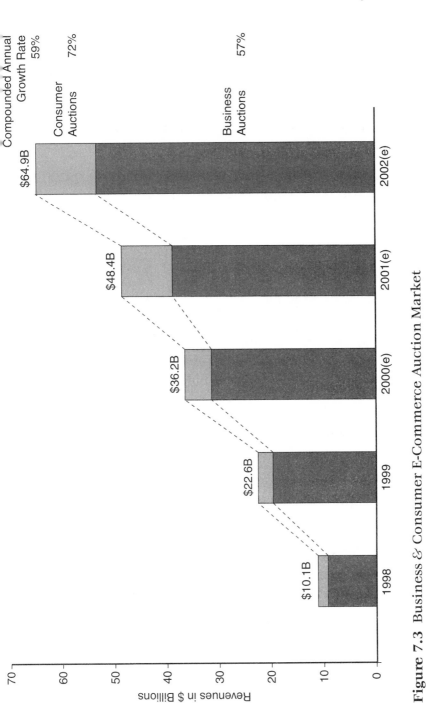

Figure 7.3 Business & Consumer E-Commerce Auction Market

Sources: Business auctions: Varda Lief, Blane Erwin, and Mary Modahl, "Internet Auctions," *The Forrester Report*, March 1998; Consumer Auctions: Evie Black Dykema, "Consumers Catch Auction Fever," *The Forrester Report*, March 1999.

price they wish to pay for items ranging from airline tickets and hotel rooms to mortgages, cars, and groceries. If the seller accepts, the consumer can rejoice.

While a well-conceived idea, the problem with this model for now, in my opinion, is that it is able to match only a small portion of buyers to sellers from the overall pool of bids it receives. In some cases, PriceLine.com itself makes up the difference between a bid and the seller's asking price for an airline ticket, doing so on the grounds it helps build customer loyalty. However, as William Shatner says, ultimately PriceLine.com could be big . . . really big!

■ THE INTERNET'S OFFSPRING

Despite the popularity of online shopping, trading, and auctioneering, Internet experimentation has conjured up new pathways for the medium that are totally off-limits to consumers. Intranets and extranets are being driven by the large business and corporate sector, which is proving to be the real mover and shaker when it comes to Internet development.

➤ Intranets

Intranets are typically internal networks that are carved out of the Internet. Representing the next stage of Internet customization, they employ the open standards Internet protocol as their transmission standard, but take place behind secure firewalls so that only authorized users have access. Company after company is building intranets to distribute information, share knowledge, and speed the flow of data among offices that are often continents apart. Even in today's client-server-focused environment, intranets are winning out because of their relative speed, simple user interface, and ease of deployment.

An intranet can provide human resources with an effective online vehicle enabling employees to upgrade or change their benefits package, for example, or could allow scientists and engineers to exchange information along with complex drawings and images on specific projects. Intranets are also irrevocably extending the walls of the corporation, creating a virtual work environment in which employees can access a full complement of tools whether they are at the office, traveling, or working at home.

KPMG has been cited by no less an authority than Microsoft's Bill Gates as a national leader in intranet development. Through its KWorld environment, the company has created a cutting-edge architecture for browser-based knowledge sharing and the collaboration of individuals and client teams located virtually anywhere in the world. In sum, KWorld is a way for KPMG professionals to access the intellectual capital of the entire firm, including vital information about products, clients, competitors, markets, and best practices. KWorld also reaches out to KPMG clients. Through KClient, its extranet application, information can be disseminated to clients worldwide.

KWorld's innovative approach to network architecture is founded on the notion that the Internet, intranet, and extranet are not three separate entities, but one integrated technology supported by the IP platform. KWorld demonstrates how efficiencies can actually be improved by integrating privately operated wide area networks and local area networks with the public switched network to meet the information needs of a diverse constituent base.

➤ Extranets

Extranets are extensions of intranets, created when a business opens up its internal network to select business partners. This allows suppliers, distributors, and other authorized users to connect to the company's network over the Net, or through a virtual private network that offers characteristics of both private and public networks. Some extranets are huge. Hitachi's, for example, embraces over

2,100 companies, while Ford Motor Company's provides connectivity to over 120,000 workstations.

Extranets are growing as aggressively as intranets, and for good reason. They are being used to develop more intimate business links among partners, pushing the envelope when it comes to sharing ideas and data, and collaborating on projects other than design and development. Another vital area in which extranets are starting to excel is purchasing. Company buyers equipped with browsers are discovering they can go out over the extranet (and Internet) and realize substantial savings by comparison shopping among approved suppliers. Orders and payments are done electronically and special software can ensure that purchases above a specified dollar threshold are routed to the appropriate managers for their approval.

General Electric, for example, created the Trading Process Network (TPN), a giant electronic bazaar that includes a dozen large buyers and over 2,000 suppliers. In a recent year, GE alone bought more than $1 billion in goods and services through this extranet and expects to save some $500 million over the next three years. Boeing managers have also seized the initiative, launching no less than 75 extranet projects designed to eventually save the company millions of dollars through efficiencies in a host of areas. They range from new ways to distribute airplane service bulletins to the sharing of massive online databases tracking the history of every plane Boeing sells to electronically sending required document to the federal government.

■ A NEW INTERNET TAKES SHAPE

Internet experimentation is not only producing new models to enhance e-commerce and business communication, it's producing an entirely new Internet. Development of Internet 2—a next-generation version that will allow computers to share data and video at infinitely higher speeds than are

EDI Endures

Long before the Internet was a gleam in some marketer's eye, electronic data interchange (EDI) was serving as the workhorse for computer-to-computer communications among businesses. Today, it is used by more than 200,000 organizations worldwide and is responsible for the exchange of some $250 billion of products a year, most of it via transactions that take place over dedicated, leased telephone lines using standard electronic message formats.

EDI has indeed enjoyed a long and successful run. It has helped businesses realize substantial cost savings over manual paper transactions, increased data accuracy, and heightened productivity. Above all, EDI has opened the door to immediate response time to orders and inquiries which, in turn, has made possible such groundbreaking developments as same-day shipments and just-in-time inventory management systems.

Although it is still going strong after decades of use, EDI's limitations are now more obvious than ever. It is, after all, costly, inflexible, and dated technology that effectively shuts out millions of potential small business users.

Enter the Internet, which is completely transforming the notion of business-to-business communication. Weighing in at about one-tenth the cost of EDI over dedicated lines, the universally accessible Internet greatly lowers the barriers to adoption for both companies and their customers. Boeing Company, for example, experienced a five-fold increase in customers using its parts ordering system when it switched from an EDI to an Internet-driven system. National Semiconductor Corporation is saving its distributors approximately $20 million annually by enabling them to order products online. The reigning monarch over this new business-to-business e-commerce model, however, is Cisco Systems, which sells more than three-quarters of its $5 billion worth of goods a year over the Internet.

now available on the "commodity Internet"—is under way. A prototype is already linking some 80 universities around the country, enabling them to share information, collaborate on research, and work out the kinks in the system, much as they did with the original Internet in the 1970s. The enormous bandwidth of Internet 2 will make full-motion, real-time video over the Internet a reality, spawning such applications as video telephony, remote medical imaging, and long-distance learning. Internet 2 is also expected to be a much more secure and reliable network.

Serving as the backbone for Internet 2, which is receiving support from both the government and private business sectors, is Qwest Communications International's high-capacity network. Known as Abilene, this network employs leading-edge fiber and routing technologies that have the potential to relay data at 45,000 times the speed of a typical 56K home computer modem. That capacity will enable the Internet to handle the kinds of complex tasks it can't come close to touching now, like allowing researchers continents apart to communicate via videoconferencing while accessing and sharing vast databases and virtual libraries.

Internet 2 currently is the province of universities only, but it could well power the next-stage commercial Internet for hundreds of millions of users. And that would take a tremendous burden off the shoulders of its beleagured predecessor, which was never designed to handle the armies of users and deluge of data that confront it regularly. Internet 2 will indeed make the network more robust than ever, providing for the integration of data, voice, and video in a way that will finally bring the long-promised dream of multimedia to life.

Chapter 8

Building the Network of the Future

The first 75 years were easy. The public switched network provided the main thoroughfare for the nation's telephone traffic. Twisted-pair wires relayed voice transmission over the network, with compatible switching equipment and common standards paving the way. Rounding out this tableau were the government regulators, who determined the prices that telephone companies could charge, and the profits they could make. It was, in short, a world of great predictability and structure.

That universe is changing at a rate no one could have imagined 50—or even 10—years ago. What has begun is one of the most enormous construction projects in history—a project so formidable in its design, scope, and promise that there are few benchmarks in history to even compare it to. The communications megahighway that's starting to take shape is not simply a new lane or two grafted onto the telephone concourse of old. It's an entirely new swath of territory that's being cleared to make way for a gleaming new network replete with high-speed lanes for transport and carefully engineered on ramps allowing access to a bold new world of information, services and entertainment.

What will this digital megahighway ultimately look like? Answer: unlike anything we've seen in the past.

■ THE CONVERGENT NETWORK

At its most basic transmission level, it will constitute a virtual network that will not be owned or controlled by any one communications entity; rather, it will represent a commonality of all the major carriers. Through open standards and open architecture, thousands of proprietary networks around the world will meld, forming a seamless virtual network with the ability to offer access to anyone, anywhere, anytime.

The network of the future will also be a composite of diverse communications technologies. The debates that are currently raging—cable versus DSL, wireline versus wireless, PCS versus cellular—completely miss the point: The network of the twenty-first century will represent a convergence of *all* of these technologies, with no one emerging as a clear-cut winner. This integrated digital network will have the ability to deliver voice, data, and video transmission to the home or office in a way that provides optimal functionality and cost. One data application might travel via wireless, for example, and another over wireline, depending on which medium can offer the best economies along with the highest speed and most robust service.

■ INTELLIGENCE WILL MAKE THE DIFFERENCE

If transport over the network of the future provides little room for differentiation among communications providers, there is one area that will make them as different as night and day. It is the area of network intelligence. No longer will communications companies just distribute information, or offer up content like entertainment programming, online shopping, and stock trading, over the network's high-speed lanes. By providing portals that serve as the powerful on ramps to the communications mega-highway, they will be able to offer their customers access to a new generation of services driven by intelligence embedded in the network. This intelligence will bestow on the network an intriguing mix of roles and responsibilities. Instead of just transmitting information, it will be able to listen to a user's request, find the best source of information, and come back with an answer. Try doing that with the public switched network!

Behind the network's growing intelligence lies a very strong collaborative partner: software. In fact, the line of demarcation between the two will become virtually indistinguishable. Software will no longer be a purchasable item at the store, but rather a service that resides on the network for which individuals will pay usage or transaction fees. As a result, software programs will be as easy to obtain as turning on your PC or hand-held device. Not only that, they will become much more affordable and easier to use and support as standardized, simplified packages begin to replace many of the complex custom programs of the past.

For communications companies, the intelligent network will trigger a multibillion-dollar market of applications development and support as well as network-based fees and royalties. Bottom line: How will this impact users like me?

Suppose I've formed a consulting company and now find it necessary to surround myself with essential services: an accounts payable/accounts receivable system, general ledger, and so on. I start shopping around for systems to handle these vital chores, until a friend tells me my local phone company may be able to help. So I log onto its web site and find an entire page of useful services for start-up businesses like mine. Among them is general accounting services. I click on and discover I can acquire from my friendly phone company a fully configured set of books, complete with a P&L statement tailored to consulting firms like mine. Not only does this capability enable me to accurately track my hours along with receivables, it allows me to actually bill my clients.

But even better news is yet to come. Since this financial suite of services is made possible by software that is downloaded to my computer over the Internet, I can be up and running in a matter of hours. The cost is enticing, too, especially for a bootstrap operation like mine. Instead of laying out hundreds and potentially thousands of dollars for a business accounting system, I pay my phone company a modest monthly fee to, in essence, lease the software. The network has become a true business partner.

To be sure, the intelligent network will change forever the way information is managed and processed both at home and at work. In the workplace, it will enable client-server architecture to enter an important new phase in its meteoric growth. Intelligence built into the network will obviate the need for powerful server machines as part of the distributive computing environment. Instead, users will log on to the network for whatever program or functionality they need, from Windows to spreadsheet to specialized applications. With networks handling the processing, computers will become little more than fancy communication tools. The hierarchical client-server structure will disappear and in its place will emerge a new order of direct and open communications between countless pieces of hardware—all plugged into the network.

Increasing the utility of the intelligent network will be a multitude of ways in which it can be accessed. Users will be able to surf the web from the convenience of their living room TV, for instance. On the road, they will be able to use such portable products as cell phones and hand-held personal communication devices to access the Net. Even devices like refrigerators will have links to the Internet so they can be constantly monitored and, as part of one novel application, have groceries automatically reordered as they become depleted.

Clearly, the intelligent network will have a good deal to say about how we manage and conduct our day-to-day lives.

■ REDEFINING THE END POINTS

As the megahighway evolves, the traditional network end points will also radically change. No longer will the fabled "last mile" be defined only as the link between the local telephone company central switching office and the home. There will now be a "final last mile"—the extra mile—in which the network will reach into and extend *throughout* my home.

Making this possible will be the home area network, a small-scale local area network that links and invests a new level of functionality among the convoy of digital devices occupying my home, from computing to home maintenance/automation to entertainment. For starters, the home area network will allow my entire family to share Internet access via a single cable line and enjoy "always on" connections—no small deal since all family members have their own PC s and feverishly use them to pay bills, check e-mail, make dinner reservations, and handle scores of other daily tasks. But that's only the beginning of what the home area network can do. With its built-in intelligence, it will also enable dumb devices scattered throughout my home—like VCRs, thermostats, and appliances—to access and interact with Internet-based applications. For example, the intelligent home network will connect my heating and electrical systems to the local public utility. Why is this important? Because the power company will grant me a 20% discount on my monthly bills in return for allowing them to adjust my energy consumption during peak periods of usage. In the field of entertainment, the home area network will allow my real pride and joy—a state-of-the-art home theater system—to automatically access the web to achieve the optimum surround-sound setting every time I settle into my easy chair for some pleasurable listening.

■ HOW THE NETWORK IS EVOLVING

Visionary as it seems, the communications megahighway is fast becoming reality, with service providers in the United States alone spending tens of billions of dollars on its superstructure. Already, the broad outlines of that extraordinary venture are taking shape at three different levels: transmission, content, and intelligent applications. Following is a description of the key activities at each level, and how they're helping to define the network of the future.

➤ Transmission

Even at this most basic network level, the changes are huge, fueled by the explosive growth of the Internet. Ground is being broken for a facility that is infinitely more open and accessible for millions of current and future users. Indeed, the virtual network that's gradually taking shape is using universal standards and protocols to enfranchise the widest possible audience. And while the ultimate structure of this roadway is yet to be determined, we already know what one of its key components will be: the Internet protocol.

IP is a form of packet switching that's being used by the Internet to transmit digital information across the high-speed fiber trunk lines that serve as the network backbone for all Internet traffic. Packet switching is a fast and economical method of sending small bursts or "packets" of data over a specially switched communications network to their destination, where they are reassembled with other message components. Significantly, packet-based IP is the standard that a growing number of communications providers have selected to drive their global networks into the twenty-first century.

One such provider is AT&T, which is leading the cable industry as it collectively spends some $33 billion to upgrade its plant in the expectation it will become the primary transmission lane for Internet-bound and other types of digital traffic. The local phone companies are readying their own express lane, digital subscriber line (DSL), to compete with cable and provide the bandwidth needed to accommodate the deluge of services that the digital revolution holds in store.

➤ Content

The Internet is again paving the way in the area of content. It is opening the door to an onrush of new interactive services, information, and applications that are multiplying daily—and turning the network into much more than a transmission vehicle. Stockholder meetings, TV programming, downloadable music, remote medical diagnosis, instant opinion surveys—you name it and it's probably happening, or will happen, on the Net.

Much of the unfolding content is commercial, which is not surprising, inasmuch as advertising and marketing dollars are footing a good deal of the bill for maintaining and growing the web. Yahoo!'s purchase of Broadcast.com—a major provider of streaming media—makes eminent sense in light of the fact real video and audio will in all likelihood be the next advertising bolt to strike the Internet. The Yahoo!-Broadcast.com combination could well be a leader when it comes to shaping the future of Internet advertising.

While many observers look upon the content that exists today as decidedly superficial, the lessons being learned along the way are extremely important. They are helping to determine the structure—and frame the issues—for the network of the future.

➤ Intelligent Services

There's no finer example of how the intelligent network is evolving than high-powered search engines like Ask Jeeves (www.ask.com). Ask the helpful butler Jeeves to get you the weather in Chicago, for example, or the name of a five-star hotel in downtown Los Angeles, or the square mileage of Pago Pago, and he'll faithfully do just that. Ask Jeeves is a next-generation search engine that lets the user pose questions in natural language rather than keywords. More important, though, this portal hints at the vast potential of the network to gather, interpret, and deliver information requested by users in an outpouring of fields.

The desire to turbocharge the network by allowing intelligent applications to ride on its back is behind the growing movement by communications service providers to implement the Internet protocol standard. Level 3, for example, has embraced IP as the dominant voice and data architecture for the future. In the process, this carrier has attracted the attention of the financial community by building out a privately managed IP network that is primarily focused on the business market. Even more specifically, Level 3 plans to sell voice and data services on a wholesale basis to other carriers and companies who will actually be buying access to its IP network.

Qwest Communications, too, is focused on IP as the foundation for a barrage of intelligent network offerings. Recognizing that his company's future must consist of more than just selling bandwidth, President Lewis Wilks has formed an alliance with Microsoft in which the latter is pumping some $200 million into the company so the two can create a viable business managing and updating key applications for mobile executives over the Internet (see Figure 8.1 for a complete listing of Microsoft's investments in the communications industry over the past three years). These applications include e-mail, database access, and portfolio management. Moreover, Qwest will soon be operating some seven web hosting centers. Web hosting consists of storing a customer's web site on a powerful server machine, which has a permanent connection to the Internet.

Interestingly, the buildout of private IP networks by both Level 3 and Qwest Communications is prompting the major long-distance carriers to intensify development of

Company	Country	Year	Amount Invested	Type of Investment	
Jato Communications	U.S.	2000	$10 million	Investment	○
Winstar	U.S.	1999	$900 million with consortium	Investment	○
Asia Global Crossing	Japan	1999	$200 million	Investment	○
Organizcoes Globo	Brazil	1999	$126 million	Investment	○
DSL.net	U.S.	1999	$15 million	Investment	○
STNC Ltd.	U.K.	1999	Small	Acquisition	○
Rogers Communications	Canada	1999	$400 million	Investment	○
Concentric Network	U.S.	1999	$50 million	Investment	○
Nextel	U.S.	1999	$600 million	Investment	○
AT&T	U.S.	1999	$5 billion	Investment	○
NorthPoint Communications	U.S.	1999	$30 million	Investment	○
Portugal Telecom	Portugal	1999	$30 million	Investment	○
Rhythms	U.S.	1999	$30 million	Investment	○
United Pan-European Communications	Netherlands	1999	Undisclosed	Investment	○
Qwest	U.S.	1998	$200 million	Investment	○
RoadRunner	U.S.	1998	$212.5 million	Investment	○
Comcast	U.S.	1997	$1 billion	Investment	○
Web TV Networks	U.S.	1997	$425 million	Acquisition	○

Figure 8.1 Microsoft's Communications Industry Transactions

Source: Microsoft Corporation

voice-over-Internet protocol (VOIP) services. Also known as Internet telephony, this nascent service is a long way from general availability as a result of its unpredictable quality and reliability. But VOIP could take off in the next three to five years as technology and quality improve and as companies like AT&T begin to bundle the service as part of their diversified cable package.

As the telecom carriers look to build their portfolio of high-margin intelligent applications for the years ahead, they can take heart from the phenomenal success of first-generation offerings. Indeed, revenues from services like call waiting, caller ID, call forwarding and three-way calling are expected to climb from $6.5 billion in 1998 to approximately $10 billion in 2003, according to the Yankee Group (see Figure 8.2). Better yet for the RBOCs that provide them, margins range from 60 to 90%. With roughly half of all U.S. households currently subscribing to some form of value-added network service, it's not hard to perceive the opportunities awaiting companies that are actively involved in engineering the next generation of intelligent, software-based solutions.

■ CABLE VERSUS DSL

Though the network of the future promises to be a convergent structure with multiple ways of entering the home, that hasn't prevented a number of pitched battles from erupting over basic issues like technology and open access. Nowhere is more heat being generated than in the face-off between cable and DSL (see Figure 8.3). Each side has a common goal in its sights: broadband. By providing thick digital pipes for the high-speed transmission of data, both DSL and cable will have the ability to carry virtually any form of communication or entertainment that can be digitized, from Internet access to live video to telephone calls to interactive games. But despite their tremendous

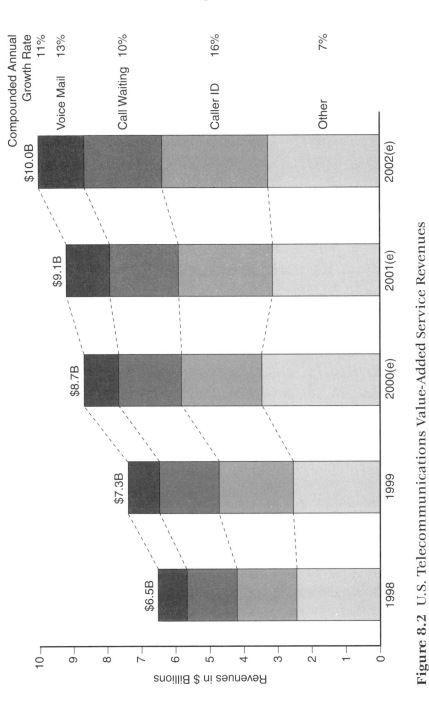

Figure 8.2 U.S. Telecommunications Value-Added Service Revenues

Source: "Network-Based and Value-Added Services: Grafting New Branches on the Money Tree," *The Yankee Report: Consumer Market Convergence,* June 1998, 13–14.

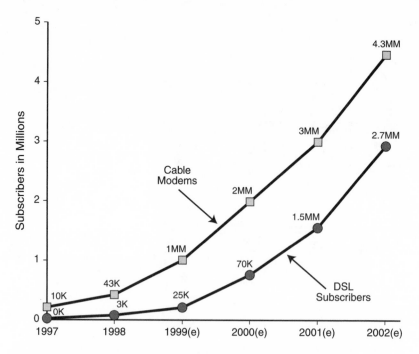

Figure 8.3 Internet High-Speed Access: Cable versus DSL

Source: "Cable Modems vs. DSL: Dispelling the Myths," *The Yankee Report: Consumer Communications,* November 1998, 9.

promise, both technologies face formidable obstacles to deployment, and at this stage no one is sure how this well-capitalized duel will play out.

Cable companies have the advantage of already offering broadband communication in the form of TV programming to nearly two-thirds of all homes in America. But this service involves a one-way flow of information: downstream from the cable company to the user. When it comes to access to the Internet or completing telephone calls, cable is being asked to do something it was never meant to do: provide two-way transmission of information. The most simple solution is to employ a one-way cable network to move Internet content into the home, but stick to the telephone line for upstream communication. These "cable return" systems are offered by many smaller cable

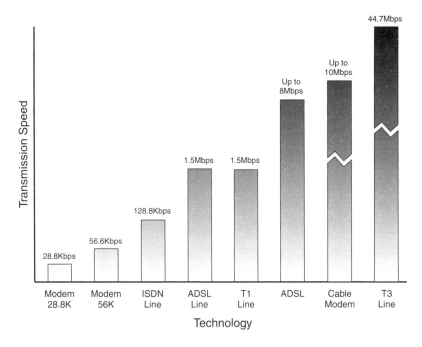

Figure 8.4 Comparative Transmission Speeds

Sources: ISDN, T1, T3: "High-Tech Directory, Computer Currents, www. currents.net/resources/directory; ADSL lite, ADSL: "High-Speed Access: xDSL and Other Alternatives for Last-Mile Access," Nortel Networks, www.nortel. com/isp/goals/hispeed.htm; cable modem: "Cable Modems vs. DSL: Dispelling the Myths," *The Yankee Report: Consumer Communications,* November 1998.

companies that have not upgraded their systems. Some of the larger cable players also offer this service in cities with older cable networks.

➤ Cable Modem

The more important technology, however, is the cable modem, which is approximately 30 times as fast as the standard 56 kilobits per second (Kbps) modem (see Figure 8.4). Cable modem systems typically allocate one TV channel (6 MHz of cable's 750-MHz bandwidth) to downstream transmission of data. This bandwidth is shared among groups of approximately 500 homes that are each connected to fiber nodes on the cable network via coaxial cable. While downstream speeds can in theory be as high as 10 megabits per second (Mbps), in practice they may be much slower since the cable bandwidth is a shared resource among many homes. (Even at that, speeds will exceed what most consumers need for an effective Internet connection.)

Another drawback of cable modem systems, however, is that in many places, they require the user to maintain a separate telephone line for voice communications. As previously mentioned, cable companies are expected to eventually offer phone service over cable wires and Internet telephony and are investing significantly to upgrade their networks (see Figure 8.5). Lucent Technologies and General Instrument recently announced a marketing agreement to jointly sell cable telephone gear so that consumers can make inexpensive calls and get features such as call waiting through their cable TV systems.

➤ DSL

The other major broadband route into the home is DSL. Developed by Bell Labs and being backed by the telephone companies as the chief alternative to cable access, DSL technology takes one of the oldest building blocks of the network—twisted-pair telephone line—and rejuvenates it so it can move data at speeds of up to 1.5 Mbps, comparable to cable. A DSL line can handle Internet access and voice phone calls simultaneously, unlike cable, and provides an online connection that never shuts down. How does DSL wring broadband speed out of regular copper telephone wire? By bypassing the circuit switches that control voice calls. The traditional phone system makes use of only about 1% of the available copper wire spectrum. Installing modems at both the customer's site and the local telephone company central switching office allows the remaining 99% to be freed up for data traffic.

DSL has its drawbacks, however. The copper wire must

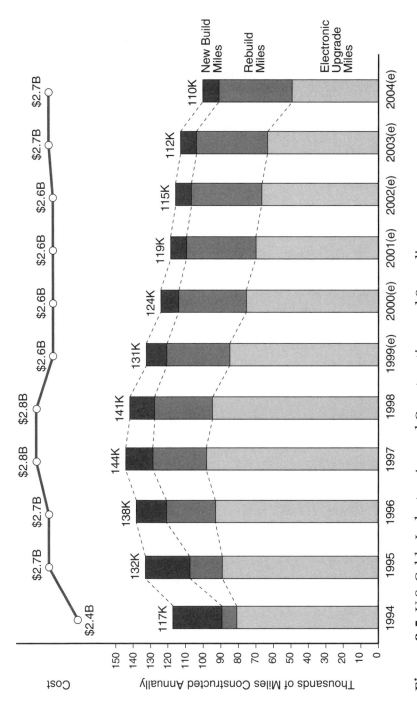

Figure 8.5 U.S. Cable Industry Annual Construction and Spending

Source: Paul Kagan's 10-Year Cable TV Industry Construction Projections, Paul Kagan Associates, Inc.

be of high quality, or the digital signals transmitted over the line won't be properly encoded. This could seriously limit DSL deployment in areas with older telephone networks and could require extensive rewiring in older homes. In addition, distortion is introduced into the DSL signal as the distance between the telephone company central office and the household is increased. Thus, homes farther away from the central office get progressively lower bandwidth and, after 18,000 feet (roughly three miles), service disappears completely. (This may not be as onerous as it seems, however, since about 85 percent of all telephone lines are within 18,000 feet of a central office.)

Who's expected to win the broadband battle? Cable already has a significant lead thanks to being generally priced lower and much more widely available at this stage than DSL. Consider the fact Excite@Home, a cable modem consortium consisting of seven of the top ten U.S. cable operators, enjoyed market capitalization of $5.6 billion even though it had signed up only a nominal 210,000 subscribers through the third quarter of 1998.

But don't underestimate the power of DSL. It will offer more competitive pricing as time wears on, pushed by telcos who already enjoy a high marketing profile among their customers. Indeed, in a 1998 survey by the Yankee Group, consumers said they preferred to receive high-speed Internet access from their telephone company over their cable company by a margin of four to one. What's more, the computer industry is expected to soon standardize a low-cost DSL modem, which a number of major manufacturers plan to build into some of their PCs.

Coupled with more aggressive marketing by the regional telephone companies, the universe of DSL users in the United States could increase to 2.7 million by 2002, according to the Yankee Group, though that would still put it significantly behind two-way cable modems, which are expected to command 4.3 million subscribers by 2002. America Online has selected DSL as one of its distribution options as it seeks to wean its 20 million subscribers away from the notoriously slow dial-up modem. AOL has been holding DSL trials with Bell Atlantic, BellSouth, Pacific Bell, U S West, and GTE. In addition, a small clique of aggressive new players like Northpoint Communications Group and Covad Communications Group is beginning to offer the public high-speed Internet access through DSL.

If a group of leading technology companies has its way, the winner of the race to bring broadband into homes and businesses will be neither DSL *nor* cable. It will be an alternative technology known as fixed (non-mobile) wireless. Backing this approach is a consortium led by Cisco Systems and Motorola. Their underlying goal makes eminent sense: provide a cheaper, more effective solution than digging up the ground and laying new cables.

Fixed wireless relies on a long-existing but little-used set of microwave frequencies known as multichannel multipoint distribution services (MMDS). This set of 13 channels, most of them 6 MHz wide, has the ability to deliver services like high-speed wireless Internet access, educational video programming, and video entertainment. Programming is delivered in a manner not unlike that of cable television systems. The head end (base station) of the wireless cable system consists of satellite reception equipment and other equipment necessary to receive the programming distributed via satellite and local broadcast channels available off the air. These programs are then retransmitted from the head end by a microwave-transmitting antenna located on a tower or other tall structure. The customer receives the channels through a small antenna, usually mounted on the roof. The signals are then converted to lower frequencies, passed through a set-top box often referred to as a converter, and relayed to the customer's television set for viewing. The downside to wireless cable is that it's a line-of-sight technology, meaning that obstructions such as mountains, tall buildings, and foliage between the transmit site and the subscriber may prevent reception of a quality signal.

The use of MMDS frequencies requires licenses from

the Federal Communications Commission. On March 28, 1996, the FCC conducted its first MMDS auction, awarding licenses for each of 493 geographic regions known as basic trading areas (BTAs). Winners have a 10-year license term and 5-year build-out period in which to construct their channels. Holding these licenses are a multitude of communications companies, the largest of which include Teligent, Winstar, NextLink, AT&T, and Advanced Radio Telecom (ART). AT&T, for its part, intends to put in fixed wireless systems that by 2003 will pass 10 million homes. MCI WorldCom and Sprint have each spent over $1 billion in the last few years buying companies that own MMDS frequency licenses, and others that manufacture products in this space, as they prepare to jointly offer a fixed wireless system for broadband delivery. MCI WorldCom has already rolled out MMDS on a trial basis to select markets around the country.

A number of major communications companies are also backing a set of radio frequencies known as local multichannel distribution service (LMDS) to offer broadband access mostly to businesses at this point. Service providers like Winstar and Teligent are using LMDS as a fixed wireless vehicle to bridge the last mile to their customers' sites.

In the end, though, the question of which technology will win the broadband battle—fixed wireless, cable, or DSL—is probably specious. The communications environment of the twenty-first century will not be dominated by any one technology or any one company. It will be a confluence of technologies and players, each governed by the rules of open architecture, open access and, most important, open competition. With broadband finding its way into more than seven million homes by 2002, there will certainly be no shortage of opportunities for cable, DSL, fixed wireless, or other promising technologies to leave their mark. One of those technologies is satellite.

Through its ability to relay data at broadband speeds, satellite could enjoy a very promising future in the Internet access business (see Figure 8.6 for some of the largest

Company	Country of Headquarters	
Globalstar	Bermuda (U.K.)	○
American Mobile Satellite	U.S.	○
Comsat	U.S.	○
Echostar	U.S.	○
Teledisc LLC	U.S.	○
DirectTV	U.S.	○
Loral Orion/Skynet	U.S.	○
Iridium	Bermuda (U.K.)	○
ICO Global Communications	United Kingdom	○

Figure 8.6 Major Commercial Satellite Companies
Source: Dow-Jones Interactive, accessed October 15, 1999

commercial satellite ventures). Companies like American Mobile Satellite, Inc. and Iridium are ready to make the commitment, and DirecTV, a unit of Hughes Electronics Corporation, has already signed a deal with America On-line to offer a service that will let users log on to AOL via their television sets using satellite transmission. The problem with satellite-based Internet service is that while down-link speeds are superfast, uplink (needed to send e-mail, for example) still requires a telephone or two-way cable line. Next-generation, two-way satellite systems are on the way, however, supported by armadas of low-flying satellites. One such project is Teledesic's Internet-in-the-Sky network, which is backed by Microsoft and cellular phone pioneer Craig McCaw. That system is expected in 2003.

■ A POSSIBLE ROADBLOCK

This is not to say the current battle between cable and DSL should be taken lightly, or dismissed outright. That's because a much more fundamental and important issue is at stake here—regulation. With brushfires breaking out across the country over whether cable should be able to control the last mile of the network leading to the home, there is a growing public chorus in favor of a strong regulatory solution. But what impact would such an action at this stage have on the historic effort under way to create the communications highway of the future? Would private enterprise beat a hasty retreat in the face of government-imposed regulations stifling its incentive to build and expand?

If not carefully considered and sensibly resolved, issues like these could impose a serious roadblock on the digital highway — an obstacle to realizing its astonishing potential in the decade ahead.

Chapter

The Wireless Stampede

How fast is the communications revolution moving? Consider this: Within the next three to five years, stationary desktop systems will no longer be the tool of choice for accessing the Internet. Mobile devices — smart phones and other types of hand-held devices — will enable the Net to float free of its traditional moorings and provide users, wherever they may be, with access to e-mail, sports scores, stock quotes, flight status, shopping tips, traffic alerts, driving directions, and much more.

What's making this phenomenon possible is none other than advanced wireless technologies — technologies that are fueling an incredible explosion of voice as well as data services in every corner of the world. Industry figures show that nearly 260 million subscribers worldwide had moved to some form of wireless communication by 2000 to satisfy their need for greater mobility, a number that has tripled over the past three years. It's no wonder that NTT DoCoMo sold more than one million of its Internet-based i-mode phones in the first week they were on the market, and that Motorola estimates that by 2005, the number of wireless devices with Internet access will actually exceed the number of wired ones!

■ GOVERNMENT-GUIDED INDUSTRY

Despite its meteoric rise, wireless is hardly the new technology kid on the block. It was developed by Bell Laboratories in the 1960s and, in 1981, the U.S. government undertook a sweeping plan to launch wireless mobile telephone service across the United States. The Federal Communications Commission established a cellular duopoly in each of 305 metropolitan statistical areas (MSAs). This meant that each MSA supported two cellular licenses: one sold via lottery (at a price predetermined by the government), the other granted to the common carrier (the incumbent) already providing local wireline service to that market.

The pioneering days of cellular abound with stories of wheeling and dealing in the license arena, and fortunes that were made virtually overnight. Some individuals granted licenses via the lottery literally walked into FCC offices to claim their prizes, then turned around and sold them to wireless operators who had stationed themselves in the basement of the building. In another instance, a couple in Yakima, Washington, who paid $15,000 for their license on the advice of their financial advisor raked in $6 million a few years later when they sold those valuable rights to a larger player.

Fact is, the government has never quite gotten its act together when it comes to apportioning wireless rights in a fair and effective way among the industry's players. When it auctioned off personal communication services (PCS) licenses in the mid-1990s, the market bid the prices up to astronomical levels, with the result being that some of the winning bidders were never able to raise the requisite money to claim their prizes. Consequently, a number of licenses were tied up in endless litigation, which served to seriously delay their implementation for a public anxiously awaiting cellular service. That same scenario has played out in other countries that have auctioned off wireless rights, such as India, where licenses were sold for prices higher than in some parts of the United States.

Against this backdrop, cellular telephone service got off the ground in 1983, with both AT&T and Motorola claiming to be first to market (the issue is still a matter of debate). But it was businessman Craig McCaw who built the first national wireless network, McCaw Cellular — really a patchwork of networks and licenses around the country formed in partnership with LIN Cellular. He sold this enterprise to AT&T in 1994 for the princely sum (at the time) of $20 billion. (More recently, Mr. McCaw's interests have turned to other communications enterprises that include terrestrial-based Nextel and NextLink, and Teledesic, with its ambitious satellite-based Internet-in-the-Sky network, which he is pursuing along with Microsoft's Bill Gates.) In addition to McCaw, other major players in the early days of cellular included the Regional Bell Operating Companies (Southwestern Bell, BellSouth, Ameritech, Pacific Bell, Bell Atlantic, NYNEX, and U S WEST) and GTE. Many of these operators, especially Southwestern Bell, GTE, and BellSouth, became adept at making acquisitions around the country to build their footprints. Bell Atlantic, for example, acquired NYNEX Cellular, while Pacific Bell eventually spun its wireless arm off into AirTouch Cellular (now part of the Bell Atlantic/GTE/Vodafone AirTouch entity Verizon Wireless). It wasn't long before the international markets were also taking off, with Europe, Latin America, and Asia becoming fertile fields for wireless.

In the United States, the duopoly system of two companies licensed to provide cellular phone service in each designated region stood until the Telecommunications Act of 1996, which attempted to promote greater competition among carriers in both wireline and wireless fields. In a move that in hindsight appears motivated as much by greed and ego as it was by competitive instincts, the FCC decided to auction off up to nine licenses in a given market for personal communication services in the 1.8 GHz spectrum. This spectrum had been largely occupied by

AT&T Wireless Services

AT&T has consistently been among the wireless industry's movers and shakers. AT&T Bell Laboratories invented wireless cellular technology in the 1960s, and AT&T Wireless Services today boasts one of the world's most extensive wireless footprints. What's more, AT&T's Digital One Rate plan helped bring wireless into the communications mainstream for consumers in the second half of the 1990s.

Cellular began in earnest nearly 20 years ago, with AT&T and Motorola both launching their novel new form of mobile telephone service at roughly the same time. But they soon took a back seat to Craig McCaw, who teamed up with LIN Cellular to build the largest cellular company in the world. McCaw Cellular was really a patchwork of licenses from around the country. Apart from size, one of the company's major accomplishments was launching the time division multiple access (TDMA) transmission standard. Because this wireless standard used only a third of the radio spectrum of analog, it neatly cleared a major hurdle to wireless development that the spectrum-hungry analog had posed.

In 1994, McCaw sold his company to AT&T for approximately $20 billion, and turned his attention to other pursuits in the communications field. Intent on growing its wireless franchise, AT&T Wireless Services, as it was now known, acquired 21 PCS licenses in 1995 to fill in its national network. When the network is fully constructed, these licenses will enable the company to increase its coverage to over 80% of the U.S. population.

AT&T Wireless scored a major marketing coup in 1998 with the rollout of Digital One Rate. This family of calling plans was the first to offer users one rate with no roaming or domestic long-distance charges across all 50 states, irrespective of whether the customer is on AT&T's network. Consumer acceptance was swift and extremely positive. Digital One Rate soon became a standard for the industry, and served to accelerate the growth of wireless among a cost-conscious public.

Today, AT&T is one of the largest cellular carriers in the United States, covering 40% of the population and providing service to more than 10 million users. Its local wireless systems are connected through a single network—the North American Cellular Network, pioneered by AT&T—that allows customers to use their phones seamlessly across different cellular territories in over 7,000 cities across the United States, Canada, and Mexico. Additional connections with international standards extends service to over 46 countries in Europe, Asia, Oceania, Africa, and the Middle East.

AT&T has also broken new ground through its Wireless Office Service, which allows customers to use their cellular phones just like a wired PBX extension to make or take interoffice calls, whether they're in the office or thousands of miles away. A connection between the PBX and a mobile switching center (MSC) gives cellular subscribers access to the company's PBX features, its internal dialing plan, interoffice transmission facilities, and private network.

AT&T had less luck, however, in integrating its wireless business with the mother ship. After several unsuccessful reorganizations, the company decided to spin off its wireless division with a tracking stock in April 2000. That move was designed to significantly enhance shareholder value, inasmuch as the market can now better analyze and value the wireless unit independent of the long-distance-heavy parent company. Even more important, the spun-off business now has the freedom to call the shots and shape its own destiny based on the unique dynamics of the wireless market.

What's next for AT&T Wireless? It is certain the business will continue to expand its infrastructure and coverage throughout North America via strategic alliances and acquisitions. One benefit to this buildup will be reduced cost of delivery of wireless services through the Digital One Rate plans. Also look for AT&T Wireless to aggressively move into data services as it seeks to capitalize on the public's growing fascination with Internet access and information retrieval via wireless hand-held devices.

microwave technologies, and once these licenses were granted, the microwave users had to vacate them within a fixed period. This public auction poured billions of dollars into government coffers, but at the same time led to a fragmented universe of three major digital wireless standards that until recently continued to thwart efforts to create a strong, seamless wireless enterprise.

Verizon Wireless

In a rapidly growing field of competitors, Verizon appears to be in the best position to dominate the wireless business nationally. A litany of acquisitions and partnerships in recent years have rewarded Verizon with the most extensive wireless network in the country.

The period of intense growth began in the summer of 1995 when Bell Atlantic Mobile acquired NYNEX Mobile and the expanded organization adopted the CDMA digital technology platform. Bell Atlantic Mobile now controlled, to a great extent, the Northeast corridor and the Mid-Atlantic region. The Boston-to-Washington, D.C., corridor is particularly vital because this 5% slice of the nation's land mass generates 20% of its telecom dollars.

Additional wireless coverage throughout the United States is resulting from Bell Atlantic's merger with GTE. Just as important, though, Bell Atlantic partnered with Air-Touch Communications — the wireless spin-off from Pacific Bell with coverage in the northwestern and midwestern parts of the country — to bid on and win a host of PCS licenses in 1995. Soon afterward, the two wireless companies formed a new entity, PrimeCo, to fill in the gaps in their respective cellular networks. In the process, they adopted CDMA technology and worked closely together on product development.

All signs pointed to a high-profile merger between Air-Touch and Bell Atlantic. But the alliance was never able to fully capitalize on its considerable wireless assets and pro-

■ ANALOG VERSUS DIGITAL

The definition of wireless has also changed considerably over the years. The term *cellular* has traditionally referred to analog technology. Basically, analog systems involve the amplification of a radio signal; in other words, they transmit and receive information through a continuous flow of electrical signals. The major drawbacks of analog systems are their susceptibility to noise interference, their limitation to one call per channel, and such networks' inability

vide truly national coverage, and that eventually led to its demise. Independent of its relationship with Bell Atlantic, AirTouch had undertaken an aggressive expansion campaign globally, and was now the largest wireless operator in the world. That, in turn, set the stage for a groundbreaking deal with another expansion-minded company, the Vodafone Group of the United Kingdom. In the summer of 1999, Vodafone snatched AirTouch Communications from under the nose of Bell Atlantic in a rancorous and highly publicized two-week bidding war that culminated in a $60 billion offer. Vodafone AirTouch instantly became the number one global carrier with nearly 30 million wireless subscribers across four continents.

But Bell Atlantic was not out of the game. Nine months later, it surprised everyone by signing an agreement with its erstwhile enemy—Vodafone AirTouch—to meld their respective U.S. cellular operations into the nation's largest wireless network. The new joint venture strategically positions Verizon Wireless in the Northeast and Mid-Atlantic, and Vodafone AirTouch in the West and parts of the Midwest, with PCS PrimeCo and GTE filling in the territorial service gaps.

Because of its size and coverage, the new entity—which carries the name Verizon Wireless—will likely be able to offer highly competitive price packages on national and regional levels. It will be, in short, a wireless power to contend with.

to provide several features taken for granted with today's wireless service, such as call waiting, caller ID, and call forwarding. The main advantage of analog—that it has been around since the beginning of wireless and is universally available—is fast being eroded by newer and more powerful digital wireless technology.

Digital wireless telephony works by converting the analog voice signal into bits of data that are broken up into small packets for transmission, then reassembled at their destination. Digital offers decided advantages over analog when it comes to wireless transmission. One of the biggest is clarity: Digital wireless better approximates the quality of wireline phone service since it is more resistant to fading, static, and general noise interference. In addition, digital offers superior capacity compared to analog since it utilizes the spectrum more efficiently.

Industry gurus envisioned PCS as providing a wealth of features and capabilities never before considered in traditional cellular space, such as superior fraud protection, caller ID, and voice mail. However, as the industry started identifying the technology that needed to be crafted for the PCS world, it realized that much of it was already under development for digital cellular networks. The only significant difference between PCS and digital cellular was the frequency in which PCS would operate: Its higher frequency of 1.8 GHz versus the 800 MHz range for cellular meant smaller cellular coverage per cell site and, thus, more required cell sites.

A third wireless technology (in addition to analog and digital) is enhanced specialized mobile radio (ESMR), a dispatch-based system used by transportation and courier services. This technology was developed by Motorola through its much older private radio business, and was intended to be a digital standard for the dispatch market. Nextel Communications became the largest player to adopt this technology, along with other operators, including Southern Company and several other utilities and government agencies. Nextel's growth came through several acquisitions of smaller analog dispatch licenses, and a large number of licenses owned by Motorola, which created a national footprint. However, ESMR technology wasn't able to live up to its promise and Nextel found itself wrestling with serious deployment problems. After failed attempts to merge with a large telecommunications brand name, Craig McCaw acquired a sizable stake in the company and took over its management. ESMR was renamed iDEN, and since then Nextel has not only managed to strengthen its position among its loyal, traditional blue-collar customer base, but has aggressively pursued the cellular/PCS market with highly competitive products.

According to Standard & Poor's, cellular operators represented more than 90% of the industry's $37 billion in wireless revenues through the first half of 1999 (see Figure 9.1). PCS and ESMR shared the remainder. Clearly, the tables will be turning and PCS will be gaining massive ground in the period ahead as the marketplace moves toward an all-digital wireless network. Hastening that process is the buildup of extensive digital infrastructure by communications carriers, which is removing the availability constraints of the past.

■ EUROPE VERSUS THE UNITED STATES

Despite the meteoric rise of wireless in the United States, it still lags behind Europe when it comes to penetration and overall network development. An examination of the underlying reasons provides a revealing window on the evolution of the medium both in the United States and abroad.

Ironically, the first reason can be traced to a strength rather than any weakness in the U.S. communications infrastructure. The U.S. landline network is indisputably the best in the world. And because traditional telephony is available just about everywhere, the need for wireless

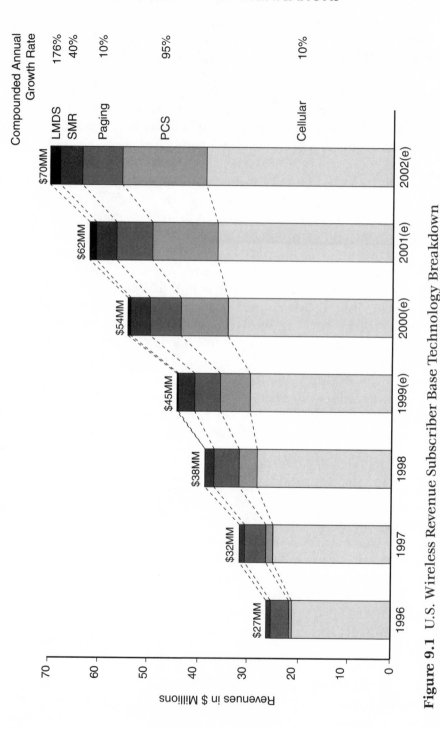

Figure 9.1 U.S. Wireless Revenue Subscriber Base Technology Breakdown

Sources: Donaldson, Lufkin & Jennrette, The Strategis Group, CTIA, MMTA (MultiMedia Telecommunications Association), Paul Kagan Associates

Cingular Wireless

With the recent merger of its wireless business with that of BellSouth Corporation's U.S. operations, SBC Communications is once again a formidable wireless presence. The new company christened Cingular Wireless will be the second-largest wireless carrier in the United States, serving over 16 million subscribers and reaching 175 potential customers from coast to coast.

In the early part of the 1990s, there were few more aggressive wireless players than SBC. With the lowest pricing plans in the country, it had gained the highest population penetration of any cellular company, and it continued to grow its network through the rapid acquisition of cellular properties. In the second half of the decade, however, the momentum dissipated. In that interval, SBC's adoption of TDMA technology was its only move of note.

SBC roused itself with its 1999 acquisition of Ameritech, which included the latter's large cellular division covering five Midwestern states. The same year, SBC acquired Comcast Wireless, giving it a foothold in the Philadelphia area. The year before, the company had picked up Connecticut's wireless service through the acquisition of Southern New England Telephone Company (SNET).

The real coup, however, is the merger with BellSouth. This latest move will give SBC/BellSouth wireless operations immediate reach into 19 of the nation's top 20 markets, covering 70% of the U.S. population. The joint venture (owned 60% by SBC, 40% by BellSouth) is designed to give the companies the scale and heft they need to be true national contenders, offering customers everything from wireless Internet access and interactive messaging to attractive rate plans and bundles of services. Longer term, the goal is to become a North American powerhouse, extending service across Canada and Mexico — markets where SBC has already begun to make forays.

On the downside of SBC's growing wireless franchise, its network is a jumble of technical standards. It may take U.S. introduction of the 3G platform to coordinate the pieces.

service has not been nearly as strong as in Europe, where the landline networks are of lower quality. As a result, wireless carriers have been able to mount a persuasive—and highly successful—campaign in Europe to draw landline customers into their fold.

Another issue has to do with basic economics. The price differential between European landline and wireless service has generally been less pronounced than in the United States. As a result, the move to wireless by Europeans is a much easier reach than in this country.

Third is the area of management. Fact is, the wireless industry grew up rather quickly in the United States, with many of its managers launching their careers right out of school. Their exposure to any other type of business has typically been limited, and that has produced some noticeable fallout. For example, as wireless service in the United States migrated rapidly from a luxury product to a business product to almost a residential necessity, the type of marketing required has also changed significantly. Unfortunately, the responsibility for that transition has often been left to managers who lack the requisite skills and seasoning to effectively pull it off. Industry investment in business research and analysis remains limited, and seat-of-the-pants decision making commonplace. Witness how numerous wireless companies have missed out on huge opportunities to pursue local and long-distance landline service as a way of migrating traffic to their networks, and on getting an early jump on the wireless data boom.

Technology also factors into the U.S.-European wireless dichotomy. While over 95% of the populated area in the United States is covered by wireless service, this network is largely analog. And analog is an inefficient, bandwidth-hungry technology. Compare that to Europe's largely digital networks, which are fully equipped to meet the continent's expanding bandwidth needs while delivering a new generation of wireless features and capabilities. It doesn't take a wireless sage to recognize that the United States must invest mightily now to overlay its analog with digital networks. And that, of course, will be no easy task in a country of its size and complexity.

Last is the issue of regulation. In the United States, regulators have insisted—unwisely, in my opinion—that cellular companies operate and provide the older analog service during and after the completion of their digital networks. In order to introduce digital coverage in cellular frequencies and still maintain quality of service, additional analog cell sites must be installed and frequency freed up for digital service. And that's an expensive proposition.

Even though cellular providers have gone the extra mile to make digital service attractive compared to analog—often offering customers price incentives to switch—adoption has been slow. If regulators had accepted digital technologies more readily, however, I believe wireless service providers would have hastened the installation of digital technology, in effect bumping analog customers to the digital world. In Hong Kong, for example, when analog service began eating up spectrum at an uncontrollable pace, the government mandated that the entire country move to digital CDMA service. And that's exactly what happened.

Regulators could also have moved faster to bring competition to the market. It took 15 years after cellular licenses were first issued in 1981 for the government to auction off new spectrum to promote greater competition. In hindsight, an earlier reaction to the market's need for that capacity would have introduced competition at an earlier stage, and the adoption of wireless would have undoubtedly been accelerated.

■ THE WIRELESS LOCAL LOOP

Beyond Europe, a sign of the changing times is that China, which had almost no wireless users as recently as 1992, now has the second-largest wireless presence of any country in

WorldCom

For years it was MCI WorldCom's Achilles' heel: wireless phone service.

MCI's earliest attempt at gaining entry to the wireless arena was through a proposed branded deal with Nextel Communications in the mid-1990s. But when Nextel raised the stakes to a level MCI considered out of hand, it simply walked away. Thereafter, the long-distance carrier seemed to have its hands tied, the only real news being the criticism it continued to draw for failing to mount an effective wireless strategy. Finally, WorldCom took a tentative step: In October of 1999, it acquired SkyTel Communications, the world's largest paging company. SkyTel, according to MCI WorldCom chief Bernard Ebbers, would be "an important building block" in the company's emerging wireless plan.

What followed several months later, however, almost totally eclipsed the SkyTel deal — as well as every other deal in the communications space to that point: the proposed $129 billion acquisition of Sprint by WorldCom. The real prize for WorldCom in this titanic takeover happened to be Sprint PCS, the fast-growing and market-savvy digital wireless communications arm of Sprint.

Sprint PCS was indeed a company on the move. It had spun off its cellular division into 360° Communications (recently purchased by Alltel), which cleared the way for Sprint to acquire a cache of PCS licenses and build from the ground up an all-digital CDMA network, known as Sprint PCS. The company had also launched the first truly national reduced-rate wireless calling plan, though roaming charges still proved to be exorbitant (unlike AT&T's Digital One Rate plans, which eliminated roaming charges alto-

the world, boasting more than 70 million users. As China illustrates, wireless technology provides a valuable medium for bringing phone service into remote, rural, and undeveloped regions of the world, where it simply isn't feasible to undertake the expensive and time-consuming job of installing wireline networks needed to deliver landline service.

gether). Sprint was also the first company to introduce wireless data to the mass market in 1999.

As a WorldCom property, Sprint PCS would finally give the carrier a wireless presence, moving it closer to its goal of becoming the preeminent supplier of long-distance, data, and wireless services to business customers.

WorldCom–Sprint synergies would have figured in another important way. Determined to develop their own fixed wireless systems for broadband delivery, each company had spent in excess of $1 billion acquiring companies that own MMDS licenses. WorldCom even created a new division, WorldCom Wireless Solutions, which began to offer MMDS to select markets as part of a national trial. A growing number of key players in the communications field are pushing MMDS as the most practical and cost-effective way—moreso than cable and DSL—of bridging the last mile between the carrier's network and the customer. MMDS, they contend, not only promises rapid deployment of fixed wireless technology at relatively low build-out cost, but extends high-speed access to rural and suburban markets that are either not served or underserved by cable or DSL.

Clearly, the WorldCom–Sprint merger would have created an entity better equipped and positioned than ever to roll out MMDS. In fact, the company projected that by late 2001, it would have been able to offer broadband fixed wireless service to customers in more than 100 cities nationwide—and have the potential to reach about 60% of all households in the United States.

For now, WorldCom appears to be laying low and is evaluating its options in this arena.

What promises to be critical to the future build-out of communications systems in Third World countries are new fixed wireless technologies known collectively as wireless local loop (WLL). Already leaving their imprint in China, India, and Eastern Europe, WLL technologies are basically cellular network–based, with the ability to realize huge economies by obviating the need to install wireline telephone service. Indeed, by putting in place a small number of cell sites, operators can achieve coverage of densely populated areas very quickly.

Wireless local loop is a logistically smart way of deploying the same wireless network that's used in developed countries for cellular/PCS services. Operationally, from a user's perspective, WLL is a lot like a cordless phone. The phone itself connects to a small, immobile cellular base station that contains the transceiver (for transmitting and receiving wireless signals). The base station, in turn, links to the broad cellular network. This architecture produces some major advantages. For one thing, because the base station is immobile, it can use the radio frequency spectrum far more efficiently than mobile cellular devices. This means a greater number of channels or signals within the bandwidth that's been allocated for the cellular system.

Another important advantage of wireless local loop is that it's not dependent on line-of-sight. This sets it distinctly apart from the other major types of fixed wireless discussed in Chapter 8—multichannel multipoint distribution services (MMDS) and local multichannel distribution service (LMDS). Both of these are microwave-frequency technologies that require an unobstructed line of sight between a transmitting antenna located on a tower or other tall structure and a second small antenna, usually mounted on the roof of the party receiving the signal. Because wireless local loop is cellular technology, it can pick up signals beamed anywhere near the receiving antenna. This lends itself particularly well to customers in developing countries because it makes it much easier to deploy wide area networks.

There is perhaps no greater testimonial to WLL, however, than the issue of cost. In the wireline world today, it typically costs nearly $2,500 to connect a single home to the local network. Because of the efficiences of WLL, and because it requires no massive laying of cable, the cost of connection per home is less than $1,000. With economics like that, it's no wonder a growing number of countries that have never known the benefits of universal telephone service are going straight to wireless cellular as the most effective way to provide basic voice services to their citizens.

■ A PATCHWORK OF STANDARDS

Not only have the capabilities of wireless changed, so have the global players. The roster of major providers now includes AT&T Wireless Services, Verizon Wireless, China Telecom, NTT, SBC, and Sprint.

In building their systems, each of these industry leaders has been able to choose among three different technical platforms—a condition that's led to a confusing and incompatible quilt of wireless transmission standards worldwide. Time division multiple access (TDMA), code division multiple access (CDMA), and global system for mobile communications (GSM) have each garnered a slice of the wireless pie (see Figure 9.2). These platforms essentially govern how a wireless network is configured and how its signals are processed. Because of the different network air interfaces of each, roaming between TDMA, CDMA, and GMS platforms can be an exasperating experience for users.

TDMA, for its part, transmits multiple signals over a single channel by interweaving them according to time slots. This arrangement makes it possible for multiple users to access a single radio frequency without interference. Among the companies that have selected North American TDMA standards are AT&T, SBC, and BellSouth. The time division principle is also the foundation for GSM. GSM was developed and deployed throughout Europe beginning in the late 1980s, and is still the most widely used

		Technology	Features
First-Generation Wireless	AMPS	Avanced Mobile Phone Service	Analog voice service No data service
Second-Generation Wireless	COMA	Code Division Multiple Access	Digital voice service
	TDMA	Time Division Multiple Access	9.6Kbps to 14.4Kbps data
	GSM	Global System for Mobile Communications	Enhanced calling features like caller ID
	PDC	Personal Digital Cellular	No always-on data connection
Third-Generation Wireless	W-CDMA	Wide-band Code Division Multiple Access	Superior voice quality Up to 2 Mbps always-on data
	CDMA2000	Based on the IS-95 CDMA standard	Broadband data services like video and multimedia Enhanced roaming

Figure 9.2 The Alphabet Soup of Carrier Standards
Source: Forrester Research

standard around the world. In the United States, GSM wireless supporters include Omnipoint and Western Wireless.

The CDMA standard was developed by Qualcomm and introduced commercially in Hong Kong in 1995. In contrast to TDMA, CDMA uses an encryption technique based on the unique signal of each handset to transmit multiple signals. It is also known as spread spectrum multiple access (SSMA) because each signal is spread across a broad frequency spectrum. Companies that have adopted CDMA include Sprint PCS and the recently announced Verizon Wireless.

Increasingly, CDMA is becoming the preferred technology of wireless systems around the world. Within Asia, the platform has been adopted by Japan, China, Korea, Thailand, and the Philippines, and in Latin America, by Brazil, Peru, and Chile. While GSM still predominates in Europe and several other areas around the world, newcomers to the wireless arena like Poland and Russia are leaning toward the selection of CDMA.

There are a number of sound reasons for CDMA's ascendance. For one thing, it represents advanced, effective technology at reasonable cost. Second, it is better equipped than any other current standard to handle the high-capacity requirements of the rapidly growing data segment of the wireless market. Industry analysts expect CDMA to increase its global market share from about 14% at year-end 1999 to more than 25% by 2002.

■ THE PROMISE OF 3G

CDMA is not the last word in wireless technology platforms, however. That distinction belongs to 3G, the so-called third-generation systems that represent a significant technological advance over current platforms and promise to take the wireless revolution to new heights in the years ahead.

There is good reason for this optimism. Second-generation systems like GSM, TDMA, and CDMA are optimized for voice services, offering only limited data capabilities. 3G, on the other hand, will substantially upgrade the data capacity of wireless networks by offering true broadband rates of 2 Mbps, compared to the current rates of 9.6 Kbps to 14.4 Kbps. Of equal importance, the 3G platform will harmonize the welter of existing standards, making it possible for a business traveler between, say, New York and Italy to receive uninterrupted, high-quality wireless service.

While the data-intensive 3G standard is heir apparent to the wireless throne, it is a good five years away from adoption in the United States, where the FCC has yet to even allocate radio spectrum to handle 3G. It appears that Japan — where the available wireless spectrum is being rapidly used up and another technological standard is needed — will be the first country to implement 3G wireless, followed by Europe and eventually the United States, where the need for 3G is deemed less urgent than in other parts of the world.

■ THE WIRELESS DATA JUGGERNAUT

When all is said and done, the wireless voice revolution of the past few years could look like a Viennese waltz compared to what wireless data of the future promises to unleash. The truth is, telephones and computers are starting to converge in an entirely new and exciting way to produce the mobile digital devices, networks, and protocols needed to deliver the Internet in the palm of your hand. While data currently accounts for only 2 to 3% of wireless traffic in the United States, according to Cahners In-Stat Group, the number of wireless data subscribers is expected to soar from 1.7 million in 1999 to 24 million by 2003. (In Europe the stampede will be even greater — see Figure 9.3.) And not

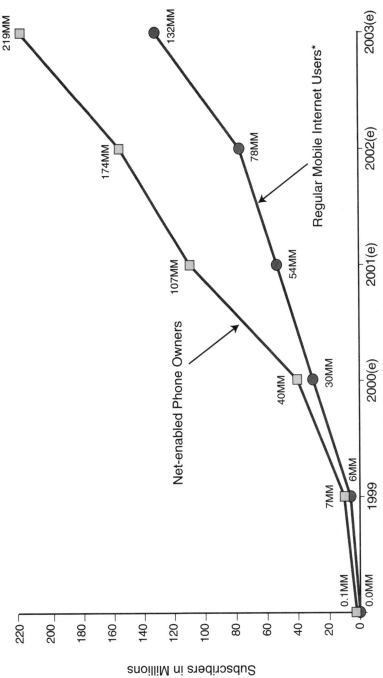

Figure 9.3 Western Europe's Mobile Internet Population

*Regular mobile internet usage is defined as accessing a mobile site at least once a month.

Source: Forrester Research

long after that, the new generation of pocket-sized "smart" phones that you'll see just about everywhere will become the most popular channel for accessing the Net, moreso than the desk-bound PC, which will quickly find itself playing backup to these tiny but untethered portable devices.

Of course, we've heard grandiose promises from wireless data before. Throughout the 1990s, in fact, wireless data was the industry's Holy Grail. "Wait till next year" became the endless refrain for a field that, it soon became clear, needed the proper convergence of factors—including attractive pricing, widespread coverage, high-performance devices, and greatly improved transmission speeds—to succeed in the marketplace.

That convergence, I'm pleased to say, has begun in earnest and promises to send wireless data through the roof over the next few years. For one thing, wireless data packet technology is improving and promises to drive down costs while driving up notoriously slow transmission speeds (which currently peak at 14.4 Kbps in most devices). The 3G standard discussed earlier will represent a quantum leap in wireless speed, giving hand-held devices a powerful broadband capability supporting video and multimedia content. Geographic coverage is also improving markedly as wireless data continues to move beyond its limited base of major metropolitan areas. As for pricing, the overwhelming popularity of flat-rate pricing plans like AT&T's Digital One Rate is turning more and more consumers into full-time wireless users as they jettison their traditional analog wireless phones.

A renaissance is also under way in mobility gadgetry, which has progressed in the space of a few years from essentially dumb devices to increasingly sophisticated and, more important, market-accepted personal digital assistants like the Palm VII, which lets users check their e-mail, plan their daily schedules and, lest we forget, make phone calls. In other words, hand-helds are becoming personal computers, daily organizers, and mobile telephones all rolled into one compact device—a trend that failed to take off years ago as the market wasn't ready for it. And as this trend continues, as the behemoth PC is reduced to the size of a box of candy, it naturally follows that more and more technology-leery people will be coaxed onto the Net.

■ CREATING A NEW WIRELESS STANDARD

Technology is meaningless, however, unless it can deliver solid content. In the case of wireless, the challenge is enormous as it attempts to replicate the detailed graphics and icons of wireline. To date, the end product has been disappointing. The difficulty of transmitting data-intensive packets of information to a web-enabled mobile device has resulted in users having to settle for three or four lines of text (with as little as one word per line) on a tiny screen. Furthermore, the number of web sites formatted for wireless access has been extremely limited. Indeed, by no stretch of the imagination could the wireless Internet experience be compared to "surfing the Net," as some purveyors of the medium would have the public believe through their bloated sales pitches.

Once again, though, change is in the air. A new standard known as the wireless applications protocol (WAP) has drawn the support of dozens of industry players who are interested in marrying the needs of Internet users to the dynamics of wireless. More specifically, WAP allows for the creation of Internet sites that are scaled to the parameters of mobile phones with their tiny displays and thin connections. WAP is particularly hot in Europe, where a survey late last year by Forrester Research found that 90% of the e-commerce executives interviewed intend to deploy mobile Internet sites, and that they expect these sites to enhance customer retention, drive incremental revenue, and attract new customers. In fact, many of these executives said they expect to reach more consumers through the wireless medium than through PCs. What do they intend to offer over their WAP-enabled sites? More than half said they will indulge online users with transactions like stock trading, travel bookings, and auction bidding. To attract additional users, they also plan to offer general content like news headlines, personalized content like stock portfolio reviews, and customer service features like order delivery status.

According to the Forrester study, there should be no shortage of takers. Europeans' love affair with wireless is expected to drive Internet usage at an unprecedented rate, with 14% of the population becoming regular mobile Internet service users within three years of the introduction of the first handsets in late 1999. Forrester believes that early adopters of the WAP devices — mostly mobile die-hards such as business professionals and trendy young adults who buy new phones annually — will ignite growth in 2000. German phone shops already report long waiting lists for Nokia's WAP-enabled 7110. The European mass market is expected to kick in by 2002 as slow connections give way to the speedier general packet radio service (GPRS) phones, and as consumers warm to the easier-to-use and lower-priced second-generation units. Indeed, Nokia and Ericsson have ventured that after 2003 no equipment manufacturer will produce a mobile phone without some sort of Internet browser.

■ A NEW GENERATION OF SERVICES

While the pace may not be as frenetic as in Europe, the United States is also gearing up to serve a burgeoning family of wireless Internet users with an array of services. A number of companies are building wireless portals that offer a complete menu of wireless applications and content. Microsoft, for example, has announced MSN Mobile 2.0, a free service that allows customers to check personal itineraries booked through the Expedia travel site, read Hotmail messages, and check MoneyCentral portfolios. A Santa

Clara, California, startup, @Mobile.com, is working with Yahoo! and others to beam weather forecasts, stock quotes, even available tee times at the local golf course, to mobile phone users. In addition, an Ontario, Canada–based company, QuoteCall.com, offers news, sports scores, even horoscopes over the radio waves, while another Ontario firm, AmikaNow!, has developed a unique service that reviews the subscriber's e-mail and transmits to a mobile phone the key words and phrases that appear important. Palm VII users can tap into a growing menu of services, like purchasing concert tickets, tracking auctions, and getting driving directions and traffic updates. An enterprising San Mateo, California, company, iScribe, lets physicians use their Palm organizers to automate such tasks as ordering prescriptions and lab tests, and capturing billing information.

That wireless data has finally arrived is underscored by the rash of alliances being formed among the industry's leading lights. They include a $1 billion partnership between Cisco Systems and Motorola to develop mobile Internet products, and the pairing up of previous wireless technology rivals Qualcomm and Ericsson to create a joint wireless standard, which will include a wireless data protocol. Microsoft, for its part, has teamed up with British Telecom to create new Internet and corporate data communications services for BT's 13 million mobile customers spread across ten countries. At the same time, Microsoft is actively promoting its Windows CE platform for mobile communications devices.

■ THE SELLING OF WIRELESS

The wireless groundswell is starting to focus attention on another transcendant issue the industry must come to grips with: how to strategically market and sell the wireless data product to business customers.

That the sale of wireless data has been handled ineffectively in the past is not really surprising. The industry and its players have been so preoccupied with wireless voice, with its explosive growth and enormous churn, that they simply haven't made the effort to understand or appropriately invest in the data side of the business. Indeed, a number of wireless carriers formed data sales forces only to disband them or let them languish in a corner of the company when they failed to perform adequately.

More often than not, companies began leveraging their wireless voice infrastructure to sell and promote data in the belief it was a logical and cost-effective step. Unfortunately, little attention was paid to understanding the dynamics of the business—precisely why people buy and how they utilize wireless data services. Moreover, the wireless voice reps asked to carry the ball had grown accustomed to selling into a commodity market where price was the paramount issue; they typically had little or no experience in selling the more sophisticated and complex wireless data product.

The result was predictable: Instead of trying to sell specialized applications, the voice reps put their efforts behind a generic package of Internet services that didn't mesh with the specific needs of customers. Detracting further from the effort was the fact that compensation levels set for reps from the sale of wireless data were usually inadequate. Even when they were set higher, the volume sold was too small to justify pushing the wireless data product.

No wonder wireless data failed to take off during the 1990s.

➤ The Optimal Sales Team

The stage is now set for a new sales paradigm with different players and different strategies. Clearly, the sale of wireless data demands individuals with knowledge, experience, and skills far different from those who sell wireless voice. It requires reps who know how to position and sell a complete wireless data *solution* that's in sync with the customer's application needs. And it requires reps who can deal with a sophisticated, high-level buyer—often the CIO of a company or his or her designee.

As it turns out, the larger telcos already have this select breed of sales practitioner under their roof. They are the same reps who currently sell wireline solutions within their networking division. These sales specialists thoroughly understand data, know what it takes to sell a total solution, and have access to the right people within the customer's organization. The fit is perfect inasmuch as it's my belief that wireless data, at least in its early stages, is really an extension of the capability and functionality of wireline service. Moreover, the buyers of wireless tend to be the same individuals within the corporation that the telco is used to dealing with on large networking and enterprise-wide solutions.

That being the case, why would a telecommunications company want to duplicate resources in order to sell similar solutions to essentially the same group of people? Why not piggyback the sale of wireless data with the sale of wireline networking solutions? This certainly makes more sense than adding wireless data to the wireless voice sales force and having to engage in massive retraining to bring its members up to speed. What's more, an integrated wireline-wireless data solution could have tremendous appeal to the customer; the marginal cost of adding wireless to the solution could bring with it a disproportionately higher return on investment.

➤ Selling the Solution

The need for an applications or business solutions approach to the sale of wireless data cannot be overemphasized. In today's complex corporate world, buyers not only desire but demand that communications suppliers understand the intricacies of their business. More to the point, they want solutions tailored to their businesses. For that reason, a dispatch solution for a livery company must look and function differently from a dispatch solution for a heating oil distribution company. By the same token, a financial trading application for individual day traders needs to be structured differently from a financial application for retail banking employees. It's plain to see that the market is not only demanding exciting new applications, but the vertical sale of these tailored solutions.

Hence the overwhelming need for a strong and specialized team of sales reps with the knowledge and skills to close these complex deals. When it comes to wireless data, they must know how to sell more than just a product and more than just a generic application. To be successful, they must be focused on a total solutions approach that demonstrates to businesses how this revolutionary new medium can help them perform better and smarter than ever before.

Chapter

10

The Twelve Commandments of the Communications Megahighway

Like all massive construction projects, highways take years to build and place extraordinary demands on their creators. The communications megahighway is no exception. It is a vast and complex undertaking — much more so than originally anticipated — that will ultimately consume hundreds of billions of dollars and have a significant impact on the development of the global economy. There is much that can go wrong along the way, however. And not every company with a current stake in the initiative will be around at the time of completion. The good news, though, is that there are important lessons to be learned along the way. I've tried to shed some light on them during the course of this book. Because they are so critical to the outcome of the enterprise under way, I've decided to encapsulate them in the following 12 points. You might call them the Twelve Communications Commandments on the road to making the long-promised digital dream a reality.

■ FIRST COMMANDMENT

Instead of targeting their best customers to determine future network opportunities, telecom companies should zero in on innovators who use their networks in different and unique ways.

This will represent a major shift in thinking for an industry that has traditionally relied on the biggest and most advanced customers to steer it to promising new product and service opportunities for the long term. More often than not, this approach has resulted in incremental change. Incremental change, however, will fall woefully short of the mark in an industry that is traveling at warp speed. To stay ahead of aggressive, fleet-footed new competitors that are determined to leapfrog the industry, service providers must be prepared for massive change that will move them appreciably closer to where they want to be in another 3, 5, or even 10 years.

Communications service providers can accomplish this feat by learning to identify and work closely with innovators who use their services—or other services like them—in novel new ways. These innovators may have made the network more robust by adding intelligent applications, for instance, or by upgrading the computer interface. The important point is that these leading-edge users are often better equipped than even the best and brightest customers to provide valuable input and revealing insights into future network needs and cost-effective ways to meet them. Imagine the rewards that could accrue to that telecom carrier that demands of its sales people, "Give me a list of all the new and exciting ways in which your customers are using our network." Indeed, by drawing a distinction between customers and innovators and learning to focus heavily on the latter, communications service providers will be taking a big step toward optimizing their future network opportunities.

■ SECOND COMMANDMENT

Realize that intelligent applications on the network represent the next major development stage, and communications service providers that continue to dwell on content will find themselves left behind in the competitive dust.

Under the new paradigm, the network will do more than just transmit and offer up entertainment and information content to customers. It will become an intelligent, interactive partner that *listens* to their requests, then searches for and brings back information from the best available source. Clearly, the most profitable and dynamic opportunities for communications service providers in the period ahead will lie not in the area of content, but in marrying intelligent services and applications to their network infrastructure.

Given the extraordinary potential, telecom companies should make every effort, I firmly believe, to take control of these software-driven applications rather than hastily hand them off to Internet service providers or others who proceed to build intelligent systems around their networks. Some companies have already gotten the message. Qwest Communications and KPMG, for example, have formed an alliance aimed at putting a host of key applications into the hands of on-the-go executives via the Internet. Strategic alliances will often be critical to unlocking the full potential of the intelligent network—and ensuring that the communications industry and its providers are fully prepared for the next major step after content.

■ THIRD COMMANDMENT

If the traditional communications service providers are going to survive, they will have to turn their business model upside-down, even if that means going at loggerheads with their shareholders.

It's clear that the winners in the new world of communications will be those companies that can think outside the box. More to the point, it will be those service providers that are fully prepared for and able to accommodate quantum change in virtually every aspect of their business, from planning to hiring to customer service to pricing (i.e., they must be able to make decisions on new pricing in a matter of days, not over a period of months, as in the past). This is not a matter of just restructuring their business, but of creating an entirely new business model that thrusts them for the first time into the role of growth companies rather than value (or earnings) entities.

Change of this magnitude, particularly in the case of the traditional carriers, will not sit well with many stockholders, whose dependence on regular dividends makes them intrinsically opposed to any sudden or wholesale change. That is a roadblock the traditional telcos will have to surmount, in my opinion, if they expect to survive and be meaningful players going forward. The consequences of a static corporate culture are easy to see: traditional Bell companies like U S West taken over by hard-charging upstarts like Qwest Communications International whose shareholders are not focused on the quarterly dividend, but on the quarterly growth curve. The survivors and winners will truly be those companies that can successfully make the transition to imaginative, forward-looking enterprise. Perhaps the best advice for the industry is this: Don't be afraid to take a radically different position. The market will ultimately recognize and reward you.

■ FOURTH COMMANDMENT

Companies that spend billions of dollars building out their networks will be successful only if they have the appropriate operating support systems (OSS) and business support systems (BSS) in place to leverage that investment.

This will require a huge commitment by the telcos to bring those systems up to speed—a commitment that few companies have thus far been willing to make. However, they must rethink and reprioritize their systems support capability if they hope to fully capitalize on their network investment. New emphasis must be attached to what have traditionally been thought of as back-office systems that drive billing, service initiation, and a host of other functions and activities. Fact is, these systems are moving steadily to the forefront and today offer customers direct access to information like account status and service scheduling over the Internet. They have also enabled robust, high-impact initiatives like MCI WorldCom's Friends & Family—which was essentially a billing program—to reshape the long-distance marketplace. The faster their operating and business support systems can be put into place, the better equipped carriers will be to roll out new network services and applications that can begin providing a solid return on their investment. OSS and BSS will also furnish the engine for customer-managed, the radical new way of responding to customer needs discussed in Chapter 6. In short, these critical systems can provide an important strategic advantage to communications service providers anxious to leave their imprint on the marketplace. But first the telecom industry must not only give these systems the respect and credit they deserve, but unleash the funding necessary to ensure that they are prepared to handle the network challenges that lie ahead.

■ FIFTH COMMANDMENT

Instead of developing proprietary applications, embrace open architecture as the bedrock for the evolving communications network.

Carriers' ability to compete will depend on the openness and flexibility of their networks—in other words, the extent to which they can seamlessly link with other networks to allow their customers to reach anyone, anywhere, anytime. Historically, much of the focus has been on standards when discussing the interface between different communications technologies and systems. But in the future, standards will be replaced by architecture as the driving force and true enabler behind network integration. Companies that fail to adapt their approach accordingly will find themselves sorely out of sync with the industry. Architecture will impact more than just the network interface, however; it will affect how different communications technologies—such as wireline, wireless, and satellite—link with one another. Once again, companies that can accommodate this convergence through flexible, open architectures stand to realize the biggest gains in the competitive marketplace.

■ SIXTH COMMANDMENT

The U.S. telecom industry has a tremendous opportunity to succeed on the global stage, but it must make sure it is pursuing the right competitive business model, or risk losing the advantage it already enjoys.

Because the United States was the first major country to entertain deregulation of the telecommunications industry, its long-distance carriers are already market savvy. They have learned how to take risks, make investments, and win customers through bright new product and service offerings. The global telecom industry, on the other hand, is still in the early throes of deregulation as a result of the World Trade Organization (WTO) Telecommunications Agreement of 1997, signed by 69 countries.

This global disparity puts U.S. telecom in a unique role: Its players are powerfully positioned to continue their expansion not only at home, but also on the world stage, where the opportunities for growth are even more extraordinary in light of the loosening regulatory reins. But to take full advantage, U.S. companies must make sure their energies and resources are focused on the right competitive process. A number of models have emerged, including joint venture partnerships involving the creation of separate companies to penetrate worldwide markets (e.g., Global One), and strategic alliances consisting of a limited number of partners who integrate their resources and capabilities, rather than hand them off to a new and totally distinct entity (e.g., AT&T and British Telecom). For the reasons spelled out in Chapter 2, I believe the integrated model is best equipped to open up the vast global telecommunications highway for its members. When properly executed, these strategic alliances have the ability to complement and build on their members' strengths, rather than overshadow or even compete with their established businesses.

■ SEVENTH COMMANDMENT

Understand the forces beyond the direct control of the telecom industry that can pose a massive roadblock to construction of the communications megahighway.

Because these forces could ultimately threaten the viability of their multibillion-dollar network investment, service providers have an obligation to understand and, wherever possible, get actively involved with and attempt to influence these potential hot spots. One such area is education and learning. The sad truth is that there is a severe shortage of trained technicians in the communications field who understand emerging technologies like IP and who can handle network integration and complex system migration. The industry must realize that without a significant pool of technical talent to undertake projects now and down the road, the network of the future could well run into a stone wall.

There are some promising signs. Aware of the gravity of the situation, Cisco Systems has created a Networking Academy to begin developing a new generation of network specialists. In addition, Motorola University has established academic partnerships with institutions around the world as it delivers the advanced courses and continuing education its employees need to prepare them for the technical challenges of the new communications era. The International Engineering Council (IEC) has also stepped up to the plate, providing through its Information Industry University Program timely instruction in the network sciences to professors and their students. This is certainly a start, but it's obvious that many more companies and professional organizations will have to come to grips with the serious talent shortage that exists in the communications field, and put their resources and reputations behind developing responsible solutions.

Another potential impediment for the network of the future is so elementary that few people have paid it any notice: energy. As the network exerts a growing impact on our daily lives in ways that range from work to pleasure, a sudden power outage takes on new and much more ominous overtones. It could shut down businesses as well as the countless devices and systems around the home that feed off the network. To be sure, the public utility companies will come under intense pressure to ensure the near-faultless reliability of their systems. In the new wired world taking shape, *any* system downtime will be totally unacceptable, not to mention potentially disastrous to the economy. The onus will be on the utilities to not only guarantee uninterrupted performance, but to meet the additional volume demands for power resulting from the soaring number of network applications. Are the public utilities up to this daunting challenge? Experience indicates that there is room for serious doubt. This, in turn, raises an interesting question: Are we far from the day when AT&T and MCI WorldCom will have to become power generators?

■ EIGHTH COMMANDMENT

*The virtually unlimited demand for network-based applica-
tions in the foreseeable future should continue to encourage
significant industry investment in increased capacity, along
with new and better services.*

The fears in some industry quarters of overcapacity are,
I believe, ill-founded. I'm basing that on the following
logic: as increased network speed and capacity continue to
drive down the cost of providing services, resulting price
decreases will continue to drive up utilization by customers. Bonocore's hypothesis, discussed in Chapter 4, puts
this into sharper focus. The hypothesis maintains that for
every 1% decrease in the price of providing telecommunications services to customers, there will be an accompanying 3% increase in the demand for network capacity. With
technology advances continuing to curb costs and prices,
and groundswell movements like the Internet and online
shopping continuing to goose network demand, I see capacity being gobbled up by consumers in the years ahead.
Thus, for forward-looking telecom carriers, the main issue
will not be "Should I or shouldn't I build?" but rather, "How
fast can I get my plant up and running?"

■ NINTH COMMANDMENT

*The extra mile within the home is moving from a telecommut-
ing to a teleliving space, and this transition brings with it a new
world of opportunities for communications service providers.*

No longer will the home environment be geared
mainly to work-at-home applications, like voice mail and
interconnectability. A much broader framework for at-
home applications known as teleliving is taking hold, and
it embraces everything from business to entertainment to
Internet access to home maintenance. At the center of this

enterprise is the emerging home area network—a local area network with the ability to interconnect a proliferation of digital devices, including computers, home entertainment theaters, and heating and electrical systems. Above all, it will enable computers throughout the home to share Internet access, eliminating the need for costly multiple telephone lines. The industry has been so riveted by ongoing battles over the last mile leading up to the home, however, that it has generally failed to recognize the extraordinary product and service opportunities that extend beyond the front door.

Actually, the extra mile embraces not only home-based teleliving applications, but the extension of that environment outside the living quarters. It encompasses students who want to get their homework from their college professors while they're at work, for example, or to homeowners who want to remotely turn on their air conditioning via the Internet an hour before their scheduled return. The message is clear: Service providers who can't see past the front door will be losing out on some of the most attractive opportunities the telecommunications revolution has to offer.

■ TENTH COMMANDMENT

For the full potential of the network to be realized, regulators should respond—but not react too early—to issues that are still evolving in the marketplace.

A good example is the current battle over open access. If the government attempted to regulate broadband access at this early stage, it could have a chilling effect on private investment, possibly setting network development back by years. A more prudent strategy—which the FCC in fact seems to be following—is to stand back and see what impact competing technologies will eventually exert on open access. In the longer run, the government may have to step in and apply strong national guidelines, particularly in light of the escalating number of communities like Portland, Oregon, and Broward County, Florida, that are imposing their own open access standards. But at least any such FCC ruling would be founded on a widening base of knowledge and experience, rather than mere supposition.

At the same time, a more proactive stance by the government would be extremely welcome in other important areas. They include universal service, where a national framework to replace the current morass of rules and regulations wrought by 50 different state jurisdictions would be a vast improvement. They also include the FCC's reviewing antiquated sets of standards that apply to various parts of the communications sector (such as cable and telephone), seeking to improve uniformity and fairness within a rapidly converging industry.

■ ELEVENTH COMMANDMENT

Embrace customer-managed as the new service paradigm for the twenty-first century.

Customer-managed represents a giant leap from the reactionary customer-care model that guides the major long-distance carriers today. For the telecom industry and its players, customer-managed means letting the customer define the relationship, then reengineering the business so it can respond promptly and convincingly to their needs.

Customer-managed will require enormous changes in the way service providers operate their businesses. For starters, it will oblige them to throw out all the old rules, and start with a blank sheet of paper. No longer will individual products and services dictate the customer relationship. Instead, integrated solutions and enterprisewide customers will become the new operating standards, with every division and every function playing a direct role in perfecting the customer relationship. Although customer-managed will represent an extremely difficult challenge for the industry — currently no company even comes close to making the grade — it is a challenge well worth tackling. Customer-managed will simultaneously take the client relationship to an exciting new level and provide carriers with the most substantive competitive advantage available to them in the fiercely contested telecom space.

■ TWELFTH COMMANDMENT

If network-based intelligent services represent the real future for communications service companies, then strategic alliances are the vehicle that will speed them to that destination.

The big winners going forward will clearly be those companies that are nimble players in the intelligent network space. The question facing telcos at this stage is not whether they should undertake that journey, but how they can most effectively get there. Do they go it alone, or partner with others? Except in rare cases, strategic alliances will provide the inescapable answer. This is why companies must start thinking now about the types of partners they should choose, and the market segments in which they should compete.

As the optimal partners for the communications industry, software, portal, and systems integration firms are beginning to overshadow hardware vendors. That makes eminent sense, given that software is becoming increasingly integrated with the network and will provide the requisite intelligence to drive a new generation of advanced applications. On the market side, service providers must realize they can't be all things to all customers, and carefully choose those segments where they feel they can have the greatest impact, along with their alliance partners. They may decide to focus on providing intelligent services to middle-market companies or to high-usage residential customers, for example, or to industries like banking where security and redundancy are critical requirements.

There are two important points to remember. First, with the right strategic partners, even small telecom players can be significant winners in the emerging world of intelligent network applications. It's extremely important, though—and here's the second point—that they act quickly, because the pool of available alliance partners is fast dwindling.

11

The Enterprise Extramile

A recurrent theme in this book has been convergent communications, and how that is starting to transform the way we do business and interact with one another. As shown in chapter after chapter, convergent communications promises to deliver an exciting world of interactive services and new-age conveniences, and do so in an eminently cost-effective way. This epochal change is impacting another critical area: enterprise systems, which is another area that the extramile is exploding into, and is the bedrock of every high speed exchange of information that takes place. No longer does systems development mean simply having an automated system to handle a stand-alone application, like billing, purchasing, or payroll. Customer needs have become infinitely more complex, and for the full benefits of the convergent communications era to be realized, I believe there must be a paradigm shift in the way systems are designed and implemented. Specifically, networks and applications must no longer be allowed to exist as stand-alone processes; they must become integrated components.

Underscoring that need is the explosion in applications that looms on the horizon—*applications that don't just gather and process information, but enable users to commu-*

nicate with both external and internal audiences. Since most companies are faced today with having to spend significant sums of money anyway on new systems development, it certainly pays for them to get it right. And that means creating an environment that's appropriate for network-applications integration if they expect to realize the trove of efficiencies and improvements that the new communications era promises.

■ A HISTORICAL PERSPECTIVE

To better appreciate the issues involved in systems development, it's helpful to take a historical look at other paradigm shifts that have occurred in the systems arena.

➤ Systems Supporting Processes (1970–1990)

Computing technology precipitated a dramatic movement in terms of how systems were designed. The concept was relatively simple: For each process, there was a corresponding system. Here, the need was greatest among businesses that did large transaction processing, like insurance companies handling claims and banks processing checks. Transaction-based systems gave these users the ability to operate faster, cheaper, and with greater accuracy than ever before. They also enabled countless other types of companies to handle the growing volume demands of their businesses.

➤ Systems Integration (1990–2005)

If the business case for systems supporting processes was greater efficiency and cost savings, the driving force behind the systems integration movement was a craving for more and more information. And no longer were companies with large processing needs the primary driver. Systems integration was triggered by the increasing complexity of all sizes and types of companies, which could no longer rely on manual processes alone to run their businesses. At the heart of systems integration were new technologies like client-server, which for the first time allowed different systems to talk to one another, and data warehousing, which allowed businesses to put information in centralized repositories where it could be accessed by people with a need to know.

Just-in-time inventory is a good example of how systems integration was able to enhance the business process. By marrying sales forecast information with production scheduling data, companies were able to manufacture essentially what they needed to meet customers orders, thus dramatically reducing inventories and improving cash flow. Among the many other improvements prompted by systems integration was enhanced customer ordering through electronic data interchange (EDI), an online system that is still the workhorse for a vast number of businesses.

➤ Network Applications Integration (1996–)

In today's fiercely competitive world of business, it's no longer enough to just retrieve information. Businesses need systems that can help them continually interface with—and be more responsive to—their various constituents, from customers and vendors to employees and stockholders. In short, they need systems that will enable them to *communicate.*

Against that backdrop, I believe we're on the threshold of a third systems paradigm that promises to surpass anything that's come before. I've termed this new order network applications integration, and the technologies that will drive systems development within this playing field include the Internet, the worldwide web, virtual private networks, wireless applications protocol (WAP), and voice over Internet protocol (VOIP). While systems supporting processes and systems integration brought together applications, process, and information aggregation, network-enabled applications adds another critical component—communications—to the mix. The result is a new generation of Internet-based applications that are enabling businesses to gather, synthesize, and share information in a host of exciting, imaginative, and profitable new ways.

Network-Enabled Applications Begin to Bloom   To fully satisfy the needs of a convergent communications environment, it is clear that the new enabling technologies will have to become an integral part of the systems development process. Put another way, it will require a seamless merger of process, application, aggregation, and network.

Though still in its infancy, that integration in fact is beginning to occur. On the business-to-consumer front, it is taking shape in a slew of dotcom enterprises that search the worldwide web for the best price on a car, mortgage, or insurance policy, for example, and after aggregating that information can communicate it back to the consumer. On the business-to-business side, network-applications integration has resulted in creative new ways to open up sales and distribution channels, and to electronically plug customers, vendors, and global partners into a company's vital processes.

This interpretation is also giving birth to a whole new class of enterprisewide solutions, the most famous of which is electronic mail. Enterprisewide solutions break down the silos within a company and draw on its full array of resources and capabilities, creating a dynamic new infrastructure in the process. Billing systems, for example, are being replaced by customer relationship organizations; production scheduling and inventory systems are yielding to supply chain management; and new service origination and troubleshooting are being subsumed by total customer management.

Enterprisewide solutions are now taking on an even broader definition. They are projecting the company outside its walls into a universe of players with common interests and goals that is able to gain strategic advantage in numbers. A prime example is the Big Three automakers — General Motors, Ford Motor and DaimlerChrysler — who announced in early 2000 that they had banded together to form the world's largest online purchasing exchange, Covisint (the letters *co* stand for connectivity, collaboration, and communication; *vis* represents visibility and vision; and *int* represents integrated solutions that the venture will provide).

Covisint is an independent company that will offer products and services designed to help auto makers and their suppliers achieve unprecedented efficiencies throughout the supply chain. One of Covisint's major functions will be to support the three automotive giants in making purchases of nearly $240 billion annually from hundreds of suppliers. Here the power of the Internet will help streamline the purchasing process and cut costs. The Internet may also help the auto manufacturers reduce costly inventories as well as respond more quickly to market changes by instantly communicating any changes in their production schedules to all sectors of the supply chain.

Renault and Nissan quickly announced their intention to join the exchange, while Oracle and Commerce One accepted the technological challenge of making the new enterprise work.

Community purchasing has also infiltrated the utilities industry, where 15 U.S. electric and natural gas companies announced plans in March 2000 to develop an Internet site to connect buyers and sellers of power equipment, including turbines and transformers. The site will also enable power companies to sell surplus equipment online. PricewaterhouseCoopers was chosen to help develop the web site, which alliance members hope will make purchasing easier and reduce order and delivery times. All energy and utility companies will be encouraged to use the site.

Another major industry that has cast its lot with community enterprisewide selling/purchasing is chemicals, where Dow Chemical Company and DuPont Company,

The "Talkative" Net

For some people, it's the ultimate form of convergent communications—merging voice with data over an IP backbone network and changing forever the way we communicate.

Voice over Internet protocol (VOIP) is indeed a technology with a huge potential payback, especially in the world of e-commerce. But to date, I believe the hype over VOIP is way ahead of the reality and that the "talking" Internet as a fully integrated, high-performance medium for voice communications won't emerge until around 2005.

That is not to say the need doesn't exist right now. In business sectors like call centers, for example, the ability to communicate verbally with online customers at the click of an icon could truly transform the e-commerce space. Market research shows that 80% of people who initiate a transaction on the Internet cancel it before it's completed. Imagine what would happen to that completion rate if consumers had the opportunity to speak to a live and knowledgeable representative who could guide them through their purchasing decision.

IP has already come a long way in just a few years. It has grabbed a foothold in the corporate sector, where Merrill Lynch & Co., for example, has taken steps to move its global network of over 67,000 employees to Internet phones. Compaq Computer Corporation is also taking advantage of technology that will allow visitors to its web site to speak live with a customer service agent. On the consumer front, major portals like Yahoo!, Excite@Home, and America Online have introduced voice to their chat rooms, and service companies like Net2Phone will route calls over the Internet from one home phone to another—sans computers.

A number of communications and equipment providers are bending over backward to accommodate VOIP. Level 3 Communications and Qwest Communications International are among the first to build IP backbone networks that can handle integrated voice and data transmission for customers. Qwest's 18,500-mile fiber network will expand its offerings to include fax over IP, unified messaging, and voice-driven e-commerce services.

Leading equipment vendors like Cisco Systems and Lucent Technologies are also major players, introducing new generations of products that allow voice to coexist with data over the Internet protocol network. Cisco's products include IP gateways that link with a company's existing PBX system, allowing it to continue to use its proprietary phone system while gradually migrating to VOIP.

Despite the intense activity that's occurring, no one has yet to achieve a fully integrated VOIP system. More pointedly, major technical issues must be ironed out before voice over the Internet will ever be accepted by mainstream businesses and consumers. One of the biggest is the quality of service, which in the case of VOIP currently ranges from poor to acceptable. Other question marks hang over security, interoperability, and reliability (remember, if the power goes down, so does the connection to the Internet).

For reasons like these, reports of the death of the traditional switched network are greatly exaggerated. With some notable exceptions, few companies seem willing right now to replace expensive and normally dependable PBX systems to cast their lot with a still unproven technology. But I believe with time, that will change. The economics of VOIP are such that few companies will be able to ignore it over the longer term. Indeed, unlike a traditional phone call, which requires a dedicated circuit to complete, voice on an Internet call is broken up into packets that share the same data transmission line as packets from many other calls. The result is vastly improved network utilization— and long-distance calls that can cost as little as 2 to 3 cents a minute, compared to 10 cents a minute using the switched network.

Companies like Cisco and Lucent are working overtime to iron out the VOIP wrinkles, and there are signs of progress. Given the enormous need for the technology— and its expected payback in terms of cost savings and customer service—there is every reason to believe that VOIP could ultimately be the convergent powerhouse that its supporters now claim.

along with BASF AG, Bayer AG, and Celanese AG, recently agreed to form an online venture that will supply the rapidly growing market for plastics-related materials and equipment. The worldwide e-commerce marketplace for petrochemicals—which go into making everything from paints to auto parts—is expected to skyrocket from $41 billion in 1999 to over $700 billion by 2003, according to Forrester Research.

Making Systems Development Work Given today's need for competitive advantage and cost savings, I believe all companies should be focused on network-applications-integration. But determining how to get there is no easy decision when it comes to complex systems development. I see six trends emerging in the design/development process that might make the road a little easier to negotiate:

1. *Applications are no longer being defined by activities, but by relationships.* Rather than design a call center as a stand-alone application, for a company, for example, a company might now treat this function as part of a much broader platform known as customer relationship management. Rather than design an independent purchasing system, a company might incorporate this function in an ambitious and tightly integrated supply chain management system. The point is that fundamental applications are being developed in a much broader context than ever before. They're being defined around relationships that embrace the vast sweep of activities relating to customers, suppliers, employees, shareholders, and more. And as that happens, systems design is moving from process-based to communications-driven, with the challenge being how to most effectively link the customer call center, for example, with the billing, service initiation, and trouble-reporting centers so that information can be liberally distributed and shared by each entity.

2. *The requirements definition mode of systems design is no longer practical; it is being replaced by an interactive model.* Traditionally, systems design has started with a requirements definition, in other words, a basic focus on what the user wants the system to accomplish. This step is usually followed by a conceptual design, detailed design, and, finally, implementation. In today's rapidly changing world of convergent communications, however, a requirements definition is nearly impossible because requirements are constantly changing. As a result, the focus is shifting to an interactive mode of systems design where flexible network architecture and systems architecture are the keys to a successful systems implementation.

3. *The changing face of applications development will tremendously expand the need for—and development of—new communications technologies.* The demand will be greater than ever for technologies that have not traditionally been part of the applications design process, such as virtual private networks, broadband, wireless, and middleware as a means of integrating legacy systems and Internet applications. Digital hand-held devices like the PalmPilot could also be an integral part of future systems development, particularly as a wireless tool to communicate with the call centers of vendors and other companies. Another technology that I believe can be used much more extensively is interactive voice response. While it's typically part of the call center space, voice response could have great utility over a full range of relationship systems that companies may be installing in the future, accommodating employees, suppliers, and shareholders.

4. *The network consulting and design process will gradually become integrated with the traditional application consulting and design process.* Go to any major corporation today and you'll probably see a distinct line

between applications and networks. Indeed, networks are typically thought of as utilities rather than partners with applications. *Integration* to these companies simply means getting the application to run over the network. I see that dynamic significantly changing. Over time, networks will be designed, tailored, and understood in the context of the application that's being run—not merely as utilities that applications plug into. By merging the two processes, a host of key attendant issues can be effectively addressed, such as security, privacy, uptime, performance monitoring, and more.

5. *Incremental change won't cut it when it comes to moving your business to an Internet systems platform; what's needed are so-called disruptive technologies.* In my experience, nearly every company migrating today to the Internet takes the systems integration process of the 1990s as its model. They believe that the technology and methodology that enabled them to combine processes and systems in the 1990s is still cutting edge, that all they need to do now is incrementally merge the Internet with their existing systems infrastructure. My take on this approach: systems integration is as dated as a 33 ⅓ record. There's a bold new way of moving your business to the Internet that's network-driven, not process-driven. The catch is that you'll never get there incrementally. You must be willing to engage *disruptive technologies.* As the term implies, these jarringly change how you perceive, develop, and implement systems.

6. *Companies must decide whether to hire people with the requisite skill sets to manage new systems development, or seek out the appropriate strategic or consultant partnerships.* With advanced network skills at a premium, the former course does not promise to be easy (though it's certainly not impossible). For many companies, partnering with third parties that specialize in network systems design and have de-

veloped a significant bank of talent, experience, and satisfied clients may be the preferred way to go.

■ TRANSFORMING CUSTOMER SERVICE

Perhaps no area better illustrates the enormous potential of Network-Applications Integration than the call center. While call centers today are primarily equipped to handle voice communications, either through live operators or automated voice response systems, network enabled call centers will have the ability to communicate with customers regardless of the technology being used: voice, e-mail, hand-held device, wireless or others that may still be on the drawing board.

Backed by the appropriate systems, network driven call centers will have another big advantage: they will be able to mix and match technologies on the same customer call, making it possible to add "personal touch" to the otherwise depersonalized act of conducting business over the Net. Let's say, for example, a consumer connects to the Web site of a sporting goods company, but before ordering a sleeping bag for $69.99 wants to know if its material is flame retardant. Not finding the information in the brief product description, she clicks on an icon and is immediately connected via Voice over IP to a live sales specialist at the sporting goods company. Not only is the question promptly answered, but the specialist stays on the line with the customer and simultaneously walks her through the remainder of the web site, pointing out specially priced merchandise and other camping equipment that might fit her needs. Thanks to the integrated magic of this company's network enabled system, a single broadband connection is able to accommodate both Internet and voice communications with the customer.

On the other hand, many questions are asked of customer care specialists over the phone which could easily —

and more cost effectively—be handled by automation. Designing the network enabled system in a way that defers the most frequently asked questions to a voice response system or to an appropriate Web site should be a priority for many system development projects.

The transformation occurring within call centers underscores a very important point: the old way of designing and implementing systems no longer works. It is being replaced by a new model that makes networks and applications seem as one, and companies that are perceptive and agile enough to jump on this systems bandwagon stand to reap some very handsome rewards.

Index